KNOW YOURSELF, HEAL YOURSELF

A Self-Help Method to Forever Eliminate All Hang-Ups

KNOW YOURSELF, HEAL YOURSELF

A Self-Help Method to Forever Eliminate All Hang-Ups

Dr. Simon Speyer

SHAPOLSKY PUBLISHERS, INC., NEW YORK

A Shapolsky Book

Copyright © 1991 by Simon Speyer

For any additional information, contact:
Shapolsky Publishers, Inc.
136 West 22nd Street
New York, NY 10011
(212) 633-2022

1 2 3 4 5 6 7 8 9 10

ISBN 0-944007-70-8

DEDICATION

Dedicated
to my children
Bonnie and Terry
and to all children
because they did not have
the Liberty
to choose their own parents
and dedicated
to all parents
who consider raising their children
a sacred contract between them
and to the creation of
a First Amendment
to the Fifth* Commandment
"Honor Thy Father and Thy Mother
but only
if they deserve that honor."
And if they do
Their names shall be hallowed forever
because only they are
the Creators of Peace
in the Family, in the Nation and in the World.

---

*Some religions consider this Commandment as the Fourth

TABLE OF CONTENTS

INTRODUCTION

An emotion ceases to be a passion as soon as we form a clear and distinct idea of it.

Spinoza

Psychoanalysis should become a profession independent of medicine, a profession of lay curers of souls who need not be doctors and should not be priests.

Freud

In my quest to provide decent and inexpensive treatment for every-one, in order to attain the God-given Right to Quality of Life, I have been greatly influenced by the philosophy of Spinoza and the analyses of Freud. My methods, developed over a period of some thirty-odd years, will eventually turn out to be the undoings of the established counseling methods of today. When SpeyerMethods®(SpM) I and II, as described in this book, become available at no fee, on every corner of every street, only then will I have achieved my ultimate goal.

The road to that goal will be a difficult one because the professional community are so well embedded in their own territory, protected by the law of the land, by judge and jury. Although the purpose of this book is strictly and only to give solace to troubled minds, I expect the psychiatric/psychological counseling community to "fight" my methods, since I am taking away their clients and their (professional and financial) status.

My methods are based on the idea that "Your brain can work for you too." All you need is a self-help method. Having discovered that, I am sure than anyone with a hang-up can fix it him- or herself, or with the help of a loved one or a trusted friend. Just turn the pages and follow the instructions. It is a simple as taking an aspirin for a headache.

To your health,

Simon Speyer

Chapter One

WHY DO I DO WHAT I DO?

SpeyerMethods® I and II . . . and the Power of Logic

SpeyerTherapy was first developed in the early 1960s. It is a proven system based on logic and common sense. Over the years a second generation of SpeyerTherapy, the Speyer self-help methods, have evolved. Pure logic of efficiency, priority, and strategy was the basis for my thought-train to develop these therapies and methods. You will soon be acquainted with these honest, no-nonsense approaches to helping yourself.

In creating these methods I had to first eliminate all my personal, genetic and emotional considerations, as well as any fears and expectations that could interfere with hard logic. Otherwise this new self-help method would have been affected by my own preconceptions, bias, hopes, rationalizations and speculations.

Yet, all logic was checked against my intuition (gut feelings about the subject) and in addition, my intuition was constantly checked against logic. Keeping these two forces in balance gave me a wealth of prescience information that I applied to understand and analyze human behavior, which led to the creation of *Know Yourself, Heal Yourself*.

Introduction to SpeyerMethods® I and II

SpeyerMethods (SpM) are based on:

Brain Science   Survival and territorial functions
Computer Science   The One/Zero principle
Holistic Health Science   Malfunctional behavior
Freudian "reliving"   Frequencies and wavelengths

These concepts will all be explained in the coming chapters.

The SpeyerMethods are specifically designed as self-help tools for people with problems that originated in early childhood, i.e. in the period from just before birth until around 3½ years of age. This is the period referred to as "Programming." It is the brain's genetic/learned survival system. The manifestations of such problems are usually depressive feelings and/or stress and/or fears and/or pain(s). All this is a result of a mismanaged, literally misguided, *ego*—which is actually our brain's guidance system to survival.

Because of the deep-seated, no longer conscious, origin of this, one cannot exercise control over these types of problems, which is the reason behind their repetitive nature. However, if one is somehow able to "kill"* the original programmer(s)—usually the father and/or the mother—the problems will eventually disappear. The SpeyerMethods will direct anyone, alone or together with the help of another nonprofessional person, to perform that "kill" and consequently rid oneself of the problems involved.

Note: Malfunctions are curable by the SpeyerMethods. Dysfunctions, etc., are not. For example, you yourself can change a tire or a fanbelt; for most other repairs you would have to see a mechanic.

SpeyerMethods are not a therapy. They deal only with perfectly normal and healthy people who happen to have hang-ups. The territory of SpeyerMethods is restricted to normal functions and some malfunctions of the brain. For all other problems, such as dysfunctions, illnesses, genetic, or other disorders of the brain, one should see a medical doctor.

What Really Iz a Hang-Up?†

If you and I together are to find the answer to what really iz a hang-up, we must base all our thoughts, our points of departure, on the available scientific information relating to the brain. In other words, it's ... goodbye soul ... goodbye mind ... and hello, brain!

This book is therefore dedicated to the down-to-earth and open-minded audience, regardless of age because a positive state-of-mind lasts a lifetime.

The words "soul" and "mind" represent very elusive concepts. In fact, I doubt they are concepts at all. But whatever they may signify they are definitely located within the boundaries of our brain. In

---

*"Killing" in this context is meant to be performed only in one's own fantasy or in one's imagination. All languages know expressions like "drop dead" or, when playing games, "We'll kill them today." Killing is an intrinsic part of brain language.
†Why IZ? Try to figure this out yourself or turn to page 131 for my explanation.

addition, the supernatural, direct or via symbolism, is translated into thoughts and language through our brain cell system. Even God and the prayers going up to Him, as well as His answers, come and go via our brain. I will return to this subject shortly.

In order to figure out a hang-up, we must also say goodbye to everyone (and everything) who is involved with or held in awe by psychology and psychiatry. To be more precise, I am referring only to those who occupy themselves with the treatment of hang-ups.* We should welcome into our midst those working in the fields of the neurosciences, behavioral sciences and in psychobiology.

During the past ninety years we have been indoctrinated with the concept that "Psychology is it." Looking back, it appears that psychology has turned into a pop concert, in which the messages have varied from unnecessary drug treatments to cultlike transference-to-the-therapist, to methods that look more like religious healing than a serious attempt to effect a cure. The best that psychology has ever done is to teach us how to temporarily cope with our hang-ups. Getting rid of them permanently—in other words, a cure—has only been haphazardly accomplished, and then only by a very few.

> Psychology never became a science because it failed to ask another "Why?" whenever it found an obvious and convenient but intermediate answer.

So here, too, it is: Goodbye, psychology—*Hello, Brain Science!*

Our Four Survival Mechanisms

Before starting the actual use of SpeyerMethods I and II, first some insight into the workings of the human brain is necessary. In order to find out what a hang-up really iz, we have to accept that our brain holds (at least) four survival mechanisms:

#1	The *Cybernetic* System	(genetic)
#2	The *Immunity* System	(genetic)

---

*Hang-ups are also known in "the trade" as strain or pressure or compulsive behavior or stress or depression or neurosis or psychosomatics or sex problems or mental tension—take your pick. And if I forgot one, you fill it in.

#3 The *Programming* System   (genetic/learned age 0–3½)
#4 The *Encapsulation* Systems: (genetic/learned after age 3½)
       A, B, and C

#1 The Cybernetic System

A genetic system, inherited from our parents, grandparents and ancestors, built into every cell in our body and brain. This system guides us to stay alive and well. It knows the *good* and separates it from the *bad*. From birth on, it sees to it that one's walk through life (entropy)* is going to be as smooth and as healthful as possible, until one reaches the appointed time of natural death. One's own sex drive and territorial feelings, as well as one's willpower and the will to live, are also embedded in this system.

#2 The Immunity System

Another genetic system. In order to accomplish this walk through life without too many health and/or medical problems, this system helps cure any damage or illness in the body. From licking a scratch on the skin to accepting an implanted foreign organ (heart, kidney, etc.), it will see to it—to the best of its knowledge and capability—that one stays alive. In other words, its purpose is to *heal*.

#3 The Programming System

This survival mechanism starts to operate about three months before birth. Its construction period lasts until we are about 3½ years of age. From then on, it works as originally programmed for the rest of one's life. It is the software for our computer brain. It's appropriately called: *Programming* (Guidance System). This survival system is programmed into the brain by those people who happen to be around during that early period (0–3½), usually, of course, the natural father and natural mother. But strictly for programming purposes, it could be anybody.

The only circumstance—after the age of 3½—that a survival program could be registered in the brain is when one is subjected to a long-term, life-threatening, or near-death experience. For instance: War (active participation or civilian suffering); holocaust; prisoner-of-war situation (or wartime civilian prisoner); mortal-fear situation; hostage situation; torture; hunger; loss of home, country, territory,

---

*More about this on page 145.

natural disaster. As a direct result of a life-threatening experience, the following usually results: fears, unusual habits, personal problems and/or social problems. Sometimes, recurrences of these kind of reactions do not manifest themselves until ten to twenty years after the disaster period. When this happens, it is like early childhood programming—learning how to survive—all over again.

#4 The Encapsulation Systems: A, B, and C

A. Archetypal survival systems, no longer needed for survival, are encapsulated within the frame of our own genetic memory: Cannibalism in order to eat; killing to protect territory or status; psychic intuition that forewarns of danger and alerts us to find food and shelter.

B. Some illnesses and diseases are encapsulated in a latent manner for most of one's life, and only become active after situations that caused severe loss of resistance.

C. Any life-threatening circumstance, experienced *after* the age of 3½: Losing a loved one; a serious accident; rape; war; fire; holocaust; any near-death and/or life-threatening fear and/or pain. The experience is then Encapsulated. Any confrontation, at a later age, with a situation identical or similar to the original trauma will again cause the same fear and/or pain. This is often accompanied by denial and escapism.

The *Parent Programming* system #3 must support and reinforce, specifically our cybernetic inheritance system #1. It must continuously build upon, support, and reinforce in a positive way the inherited biological, and genetic information present in the newborn infant. In other words, his or her built-in character all of which an infant already possesses when coming into the world, must be reinforced and guided by the parents. The most important thing that this inherited behavior gives the infant is a basic genetic knowledge of what love and security should be. Love and security alone determine survival, because without them, the infant would die. Parental programming of a child is analogous to designing the software of a computer. Therefore, the programming must be one of love and security.

It is interesting to note that the basic theory of computer science is based upon only two basic components: One (1) and Zero (0). It is from sequences and combinations of these two elements that the computer can construct and sort out any amount of information. Well, our brain does the same and needless to say it did so long before any computer. In our brain, however, One and Zero are represented by Life and Death (toward oneself) and Love and Kill (toward another). Our brain thinks mainly in terms of life and death, good and bad, love or kill. From these basic components, just like a computer, it builds a personality and our day-to-day behavior.

Our brain "received" this particular One-Zero or Life-Death method of thinking because we are an indivisible part of the Universe. The basic laws and forces of the logically functioning Universe are directly related to the thought processes of our logically thinking mind. I'll explain what I'm getting at here. Science has adapted the basic One-Zero relationship in computers. In physics and astrophysics we find the Strong-Weak forces—and in the human brain it is the Life-Death relationship. This dual physical force was first translated into human "thoughts" (philosophies and symbolisms) by the Chinese as Yin and Yang. Later, other thinkers talked about Good-Evil and the pioneers of religions named it God-Devil and Heaven-Hell.

Life-Death is the one basic element of human thought and behavior. This Life-Death, Love-Kill principle is of extreme importance, and later in this book, it will be applied to deal with hang-ups.

Now, back to the original question: What really IZ a hang-up? Well, it's as simple as this: If, during the programming years (0–3½), parents do not reinforce the genetic (inherited) program, specifically with love and security, but instead ignore it, or go against it, their child *will without a doubt have a hang-up in his or her later life.*

Before going any further, let me first give you an idea how hang-ups operate and how they manifest themselves in day-to-day adult life.

A Parent-Created Survival Mechanism (as opposed to a genetic survival mechanism)

Step 1. I love my parents.
Step 2. My parents do *not* love me.
Step 3. That hurts.
Step 4. I *can not* express that hurt.
Step 5. I wish for an ideal situation.

The Same in Greater Detail

Step 1. Every human is born with the inherited knowledge of having need for giving and receiving love and getting security.
Step 2. Every infant, instinctively, feels and experiences the lack of parental love and security.

Step 3. This lack of love and security should be reacted upon with sadness and/or anger.

Step 4. This reaction cannot take place because of the child's fear of its parent(s).

Step 5. The child will wish for an ideal love and security situation. This wish will always remain a wish. Its fulfillment is not part of reality.

Step 4 is also the "degree-indicator." A child that is able to express itself, rebelling adequately against the defective parent(s) will have little or no hang-ups in later life. Let's call this a zero percent situation. A child that dares not express itself at all, because of fear of defective parents, will certainly have hang-ups in later life. Let's call this a 100 percent situation. The intensity of the hang-up lies somewhere between zero and 100 percent, depending on the degree of expressiveness or non-expressiveness of the now adult child.

Looking at Parent-Created Survival mechanisms from another direction, we find the following facets of programming:

Absorb   A child, having absorbed the attitude of the parent of the opposite sex will repeat, in an identical manner, these same signals, feelings and emotions to others of the opposite sex when he or she is an adult. (For homosexuals it is the same sex parent.)

Likeness   Some children grow up with an unaffectionate, non-touching parent of the opposite sex. These children may encounter in their early childhood years (before age 3½) a person who is affectionate with them. This may be a relative, a friend, a neighbor, or a one-time visitor. The physical impression such a frequent or one-time visitor leaves on the child may stay with him or her forever. As an adult, he or she will only fall in love with, or feel affection for a person having the same physical likeness as the affectionate visitor from the past. The attraction could be related to: color of hair, eye expression, complexion, smell, shape of face or body, or even tone of voice. At first sight of a person fitting the profile, it's like turning on a biological switch and no reasoning helps. Such an all-consuming romance could sometimes lead to a "fatal attraction." (For homosexuals, see explanation at top).

Imitate   A child will imitate, in his later life, the actions of the parent of the same sex. These actions and attitudes observed through his senses during his programming years, (0–3½), can be physical habits such as laughter, a cough, the tone of the voice, abrasive behavior, etc. The "imitating mechanism" is based on the following circumstances: The stronger the unobtainability of the attention of the parent of the opposite sex, the stronger the need to imitate the parent of the same sex. (For homosexuals, it is imitating the opposite-sex parent.)

The "Imitating-the-parent of the Same Sex Mechanism."

Homosexuals imitate the parent of the opposite sex.

DAUGHTER

1. *Father* and *Mother* are warm, affectionate together.
2. *Daughter* observes their warmth but is not allowed to participate.
3. *Daughter* never gets warmth from *Father*.
4. *Daughter* imitates *Mother* and tries via the imitation method to get to the warmth of *Father*.

SON

1. *Father* and *Mother* are warm, affectionate together.
2. *Son* observes their warmth but is not allowed to participate.
3. *Son* never gets warmth from *Mother*.
4. *Son* imitates *Father* and tries via the imitation method to get to the warmth of *Mother*.

The Wish Syndrome

Billions of dollars are wasted each year on "peddlers of wishes." They could be writers of pop psychology books, newspaper columnists, TV and radio talk show hosts, writers and editor who contribute to popular and professional science magazines and even charismatic religious figures. There are also the "soothsayers" who use the spoken word in workshops and in cults such as the Moonies, Scientology and the like. They all prey on one's wish for a "better life," for financial and social "success" or for "better relationships." Let's state here that we are talking about a wish as a part of so-called compulsive behavior. Anyone who has a hang-up always has this wish for better things, the things he or she wants in life but never seems to get or, when they get them, somehow they don't last. That wish is an indivisible part of any hang-up. Another indivisible part of the wish is that it can never really be fulfilled and must always remain a wish.

All peddlers and soothsayers feed that wish. They all tell you: "Be somebody," "Achieve," "Do it my way" ... and then they charge you for it. And you, the unfortunate, who is saddled with this wish syndrome, you pay, nourishing your own hang-up and not getting anywhere. This is because, if you do somehow come close to reaching that wish, you will either destroy it, run away from it, or create circumstances which will ensure that "success and the good life" remain impossible dreams.

All this, because of a certain guidance system in the brain which will see to it that you follow its program to the letter (with negative results for you). Most psychotherapeutic movements encompass groups of hung-up people. As long as these people stay within the boundaries of such an organization, they will feel "pseudo good" because of their transference* to that organization. The moment, however, that they step out, or if the transference somehow ends, the same old problem-life will be back in full force, including that wish syndrome again. One positive exception is AA (Alcoholics Anonymous). Its system requires participants to constantly stay "in transference" and consequently off the alcohol.

Most religious ideologies operate similarly. Their members are constantly in transference to their church, temple, mosque or synagogue. This also includes movements of Indian or Far-Eastern Gurus. So, don't let anybody—and that includes the Establishment's psychiatrists, psychologists, therapists and counselors of all sorts, including religious ones—tell you that their system can fulfill your wish in life, that they have "The Answer" to all your problems. It just doesn't work that way!

There is only one real method to solve your problems—and that is to "kill" the culprit(s) who caused the problems in the first place, including that wish syndrome. By performing the "kill," in whichever fantasy or method you would want to do it, you can get rid of your problem. All of the above mentioned institutions are certainly welcome to experiment with the SpM, for the love of Mankind.

After SpeyerMethods I and II, the unreal wishes will have automatically disappeared. From then on, if one so desires, a realistic wish can come true. It will feel like a whole new vista on life.

---

*Psychoanalytically or therapeutically induced affection of patient (client) to his/her psychiatrist, therapist or organization.

To illustrate the typical wish syndrome let's review some ads in which a prospective mate is searching for a partner:

- A woman who mentioned in her ad that the man she's looking for must not be a "drinker" usually comes from a family background in which her father was an alcoholic.
- A man who insisted on finding a "warm" woman, probably came from a "cold-mother" family.
- A woman who mentioned that the man she would like to meet should be "honest" probably comes from a "lying" family background.
- A man who stated that he is a "one-woman man," generally comes from a background of foster homes or a succession of stepmothers.

In all of the above and millions of similar cases, the person who placed the ad expressed a not-to-be-fulfilled wish. In reality, he or she couldn't cope or live with that desired person.

This same wish syndrome is expressed everyday in singles' bars and singles' get-togethers.

Warning: Check his or her family background and if the expressed wish is not in balance with the person's programming during years 0–3½, *Beware!*

The Then-and-Now Principle of Programming

Before starting to teach you the actual mechanics of SpeyerMethods I and II, it is extremely important that you be acquainted with the Then-and-Now Principle. Then-and-now means that everything that happened to a person in his early childhood, good and bad, will be repeated in later life in exactly the same manner. Although over the years the actors on one's life's stage have changed, the acting remains the same.

In cases of bad programming the child, when an adult, will follow the same rules his parents taught him when he was little.

The same goes, of course, for good programming, but that will not create a hang-up.

Bad programming includes very specifically the mental and often physical pain that accompanies all adult emotional actions and reactions. And yes, again at the same time all these pains are accompanied by that wish for an ideal, improved situation. In later life this wish, too often, becomes one's unshakable opinion. This opinion, too, must remain a wish since one's childhood opinion is based on one's bad

programming. (Quite often this "opinionation"
lic figures. Their odd behavior can usually be
were treated in their programming years.) K
syndrome. It is of extreme importance to sep

During the programming years (0–3½),
molded into permanent form by the father a
degree by the environment. The following
point:

Every single normal, healthy baby is born with the capability of
making sound. His father and mother take that sound and begin
molding it into words. They start with "Say Ma-ma," "Say Dad-dy,"
and eventually the child will speak English. Now, let's look at what is
going to happen to that very same child of these very same parents.
Assume that immediately after birth, we're going to take that child to
China and put it with Chinese step-parents. This very same child with
its inherited sound from its natural parents, will then begin to speak
Chinese. This is now the way its inherited sound is molded. The sound
is the same but how the child uses the sound in later life depends on
which way its parents formed and molded it. The child could have been
taken to Holland and it would have spoken Dutch. Or Spanish, if it had
been taken to Mexico. The same child, the same inherited capability
for sound. Yet, what the child does with this capability in later life
depends entirely on who is the teacher during his programming period.

And, as it is with sound, so it is with all other traits. Let's take *Love*.
Every child is born with the capability and the need to receive and
give love. *How* it is going to deal with love in later life depends on
how the child's parents have molded and formed that love relationship
between themselves and their child during the first 3½ years of its life.
The father will program his daughter for her future relationships with
men, specifically the man she will love and any man who will be in a
state of authority in her life, such as her boss.

The father will also program his son for his future relationships with
men, specifically those he will work with, and those he will have to obey
and accept as authority figures. The father also programs his son for
his attitude towards the law.

The mother will program her daughter for her future relationships with women, the feminine world, and her son for his future
relationship with women and his world of love.

Inhibition or freedom of expression is programmed through the
parent by either instilling *fear*, so that the child's expression will
be frustrated, or by allowing him—or her—to express himself, to
be himself. The general home atmosphere the parents create also

is their child for his later home atmosphere. The child, when will tend to repeat the same conditions in his home which vailed in his parents' home during his early childhood.

All the fear, all the happiness, anything that happened in the relationship with his parents in his childhood home, will be programmed in his "computer" brain and guide him for the rest of his life. The parents have set the behavior patterns, his norm, for the rest of their child's life.

Following are some typical "text book" examples of hang-ups:

Hang-Up Number One: No Love . . . and Shirley

Hang-up number one—the most common hang-up—has to do with one's love life, or rather, one's "no-love" life.

The inherited trait is one of need for giving and receiving love, need for warmth, affection, physical touch and the need to feel secure. A child *must* know that his parents love him (her). But what happens if the parents do *not* comply with the inherited love traits and needs of their child? What happens if they don't give it what it is entitled to by virtue of being born to them? What happens if the parents deny their child its birthright as a human being? Well, then the child will be in trouble and, if nothing is done about it . . . *for the rest of his or her life!* If the child senses, during the programming years, that its parents are mean, cold, not interested, not affectionate, and they are not giving their child what it expected from them when it came into this world, then the parents have set a pattern with which the child is saddled for the rest of its life. The child will be capable of giving and receiving physically and intellectually, but never emotionally.

Shirley Meets Her Father   I have detailed a simplified example that demonstrates the basic need for love.

Since Shirley can only think in very primitive terms, she has accepted this simple survival guidance code or program:

Step 1.	Little Shirley wants and needs the love of her father.
Step 2.	Her father doesn't give her love.
Step 3.	Shirley is hurt because she doesn't get love and security.
Step 4.	She cannot and dare not express her hurt to her father.
Step 5.	He is still her father and she *has* to love him because she depends on him in order to stay alive.
Step 6.	She therefore accepts his rejection as "love."
Step 7.	Rejection is very painful.
Step 8.	She accepts rejection-pain as "love."

Step 9. She cannot and dare not express this rejection-pain to anyone.

Step 10. She wishes her father would love her and we are back to step 1.

The emotional part of Shirley has accepted this painful situation as *norm*. She will only be able to love if she is going to be rejected. Her personal guidance system will be on the lookout for the "rejection = norm" situations in her entire walk through life. This happens because all of this information is programmed into her brain (like a computer). Thus, when Shirley has grown up and begins relating with men, the same survival information that was implanted in her brain by her relationship with her father pops up and *tells* her how to behave with other men. In her computer brain, all men she likes are compared to her father.

Shirley Meets Robert

Step 1. She likes him.
Step 2. He treats her coolly and rejects her.
Step 3. Shirley is hurt but . . .
Step 4. She still loves him.
Step 5. Memories are painful (= rejection pain).
Step 6. Her wish for love remains unfulfilled.

This type of love situation is the *norm* for Shirley in both her mind and in her life. Intellectually, she may reject Robert's cold treatment of her. Emotionally, she is "attracted" to his rejection. Rationalization enters the picture and Shirley tells herself, "I don't like men with curly hair, anyhow." And she goes merrily on to the next man and the whole pattern starts all over again.

Shirley Meets Another "Robert"   In this example, trouble starts when Robert does *not* cooperate with Shirley's norm and really loves her, too. Now we're getting the following sequence:

Step 1. Shirley loves Robert.
Step 2. Robert loves Shirley too!!!
Step 3. He does *not* reject her.

We're in trouble with this scenario because an angry microchip pops out of Shirley's brain and warns, "If this guy Robert loves you, Baby, he'll sure spell 'death' to you, 'cause love ain't supposed to be this way."

But Robert doesn't give up. He is warm, affectionate and loving. He is everything Shirley always wanted. But Shirley's survival guidance code (early programming) reminds her she shouldn't trust Robert and all his attention. He either wants her father's money or he has dishonorable intentions. She will next start to find fault with Robert, break off the relationship, or make him so angry that he breaks it off.

Now we come to:

Step 4.   Shirley is hurt. But at least her personal guidance system is satisfied and in a way, so is Shirley because . . .

Step 5.   she is rejected again.

Whenever she gets the love she reads about in *True Love* magazine or sees in the movies, her early programming will always prevent her from keeping it.

Of course she really wanted to give and receive love and affection in her relationship with Robert. She wanted the same thing with her father. But coming within "two inches" of having it, her survival guidance codes (early programming) stopped her cold. She would "die" if she did not conform to her survival program.

All this causes terrible frustrations and makes her do things she might ordinarily not wish to do. For instance, she may rationalize to herself, "I'll just have sex with Robert. Sex feels good and I do not have to get emotionally involved." But how long is that satisfactory, if she has to go from one Robert to another Robert to another Robert . . .

Hang-Ups Are the Curse of Western Civilization

As it is with Shirley, so it could have been with Robert. If Robert had been programmed early in life by a cold and distant mother, he, too would only "love" women who reject him.

What makes this negative early programming so tragic is that we only live once. We also have an inherent knowledge that our love and emotional interactions are not satisfactory and should be different. Therefore, we continuously wish for improvement but unfortunately this remains only a wish. It is worse than a tragedy, it's a curse! But cheer up, you're on your way to doing something about it.

Hang-Up Number Two: No Security

Every child has the need to feel secure. He (she) needs the secure feeling of his home, his room, his bed, his toys. Security is permanency within the family structure. Some families have to move frequently because of father's or mother's work. If they move from house to house or from city to city, the following pattern is established in the child's brain: "If I want to be 'happy and secure,' I must move frequently from place to place." Naturally, such a child is not happy and secure. All that moving is disturbing. It makes the child afraid and insecure. It doesn't know it is going to some new place simply because a parent happens to be transferred; it only knows it is losing its security, and that hurts. Again, if this moving happens frequently enough, this pain and insecure feeling becomes the *norm* and is engraved in the child's programming. In the youngster's later adult life, this person will never live in one place too long. If there is a prolonged residency in one location, the adult may keep moving the furniture around just to be able to change something, because to *move*, has become the ingrained way of life.

If in a marriage *one* partner comes from a "moving" family and the other does not, the unmoving partner will not understand all that need for constant moving and will try to put the brakes on, which in turn will create friction in the family. If *both* partners come from a *moving* background, it could be more serious. Moving from house to house is not only costly, it also creates yet another generation of movers.

Hang-Up Number Three: No Communication

Every child is born with the need to express himself. He (she) has to talk, to gesture, to communicate with parents. If the parents' attitude is one of "You may be seen but not heard," or if they are indifferent toward their child, or have "no time" to communicate, then the child's efforts to express itself will produce feelings of fear or indifference and eventually withdrawal behavior. Fear, indifference, escape, and the like will have become the *norm* in the child's adult life. "Do Not Communicate" becomes his motto.

The child's early programming will have the following coding:

Step 1.   You start to say something to your father/mother/both.
Step 2.   Your father says sternly *"Don't talk!"*
Step 3.   You wish he would communicate but . . .
Step 4.   You have a *fear* of saying another word.
Step 5.   You don't talk at all.

A little girl with such parents will grow up only to have fear of talking to her husband or lover and *need* to fear him in order to sense love. The little boy who grew up fearful of his father will fear his boss, his superior, throughout his adult life. His promotion will go to someone else because the computer in his brain (the pattern throughout his programming years) will say: "If you express yourself, you 'die.'" He will never be able to comfortably say what he really feels.

The same naturally goes for mothers who are too strict. This time both the boy and the girl will have problems in adult life expressing themselves toward women.

If both parents are too strict and not communicative, the child is definitely in for some problems in later life. It has to keep its emotions inside. When "talk" is inhibited during early childhood, he (she) will "talk" later in life with the body rather than in words. Having sex with someone often becomes the only way to say, "I love you," the only way to say, "I care." When such an adult wants to express an opinion or anger, he can only shout or scream and/or use his muscles. And if, as a child, this person was not creative or didn't love animals, he will walk through life giving everyone the impression that he is hard and cold.

There are obviously many, many more hang-ups to classify. I will go into detail about the most serious ones. Throughout a person's entire life most thoughts and behavior are the results of inherited traits and *how* they were programmed by the parents. It is important to remember that our early programming determines whether or not we are predisposed toward liking or disliking certain people, things or even certain information.

One-Parent Hang-Up

Some children grow up with only one parent, usually the mother.

1. Girl—With No Father   A girl who grows up without a father does not receive a father image in her brain. If, up to the age of 3½ she has had *no* real or substitute father figure, *no* proper love image is set in her brain on her "love" program. Her early programming is completed at age 3½ and all subsequent father-type images enter a different part of the brain and will be treated just like any other regular memory.

Even when a father figure enters her life after 3½, she will still have an empty father-chip in her programming which will cause her to subconsciously relate poorly to men all her adult life.

If a child grows up in a decent but fatherless home and is well protected by a loving and caring mother, the child will still feel the void of not having a father. This is a result of one's genetic knowledge. And even if a father figure arrives after age of 3½, the empty gap (before 3½) can never be filled. No one can put a father into those empty cells, ever.

As a woman, she will, therefore, never really "know" *how* to love a man. She will judge a man with Survival #3, which happens to be empty. Therefore, she will be attracted sexually or intellectually but will never feel the emotional part of love. Because of this lack of information, she will never be sure of her love and her lover. She will either reject every man or love indiscriminately. In either case, she will not be able to use proper judgment. The only thing she can count on is luck or, as some call it, Fate.

It is therefore of extreme importance to the small child that the mother sees to it that there is some sort of male authority figure around. Perhaps a stepfather, a steady boyfriend, Grandpa, Uncle Bill or a neighbor. Lots of grandfathers have been great father images for lots of little children, sometimes even a better one than the real father who somehow disappeared from the child's life at the wrong time.

2. Boy—With No Father   If a boy grows up without his natural or a substitute father until the age of 3½, he will have a problem in later life accepting any form of authority. He will develop problems in trusting and respecting men and developing close solid friendships with them. He may also develop problems with the law or with following rules at work or any other structured environment.

Note: A single woman who *purposely* gets pregnant, knowing that there will be no father in the life of her child, must realize that she's creating a child who will be an emotional wreck for his/her entire life! The same goes for homosexual and lesbian couples who adopt or otherwise bring up children.

One Parent Too Many . . . and Andrew

Andrew was, if not extremely happily married for twelve years, comfortably happily married. Marriage had become routine, until his wife discovered that he had had numerous girl friends over the past ten years. Understandably, happiness and even comfort went out the marriage door.

In therapy, it became clear that Andrew grew up with a mother who was not too interested in him and left his rearing to the maid. And there was not just one maid but a succession of them. His programming was, therefore, "It is natural to have, in addition to mother (read wife), several different maids (read girl friends)."

The *key* here is that his mother did not have a loving interest in her son. With a loving mother the maids would not have had a chance to affect him and be all that influential during his programming years.

The Uninterested-Parents Hang-Up

Parents who have *no* interest in their child, will end up programming their youngster with a pattern that translates to the following behavior pattern: "If you want to relate pleasantly to people, you should be sure that they do not show any interest in you. If they do, it spells 'death' and you had better run or somehow destroy their interest in you. By the same token, you cannot express interest in other people, even though you may *want to* very badly."

The Jealousy Hang-Up . . . and Beverly

Jealousy, cruelty, alcoholism—all these parental attitudes set patterns in a child's brain. If they prevail long enough during the programming years, they will become the child's *norm* in his later life even if it is against the child's own preference and better judgment when he (she) is an adult. Early programming supersedes so-called 'logical' adult behavior and generally is the explanation of personality flaws and emotional/sexual problems in later life.

For example, Beverly was married and insanely jealous of her husband. He was very much in love with her and never so much as looked at another woman, yet Beverly constantly accused him of having affairs. Not a day passed without violent arguments. Jealousy was her compulsion. She *had* to be jealous and the jealousy became her way of sharing love. It was her programming. But let Beverly tell you her own story:

"I did have a father, but he left the house when I was four. My father had a very strong sexual attraction to my mother. And for me, too. I felt it and could see it in his eyes even when I was a baby, though he never touched me; I am sure of that. However, I saw, I heard, and I smelled him making love to my mother all the time. At times I was even in the same bed with them. And I was jealous because I too wanted to get his love."

A child will develop jealousy if there is any conscious or subconscious indication of sexual interest in the attitude of the parent of the opposite sex. This attitude may be based on physical evidence, as in Beverly's case, or the result of behavior as evidenced through looks and stares. Whether the sexual interest is freely expressed or inhibited, the child will pick it up and the attitude will develop into a jealousy pattern in later life. (This applies to the parent of the same sex for homosexuals.)

The Promiscuity Hang-Up

If you see your father or mother making love to a stranger, an acquaintance, or a relative, instead of to each other, then the parent's sexual attitude will become your *norm*. And that "making love" may vary from just kissing on the sofa to actual intercourse on the carpet in the living room.

Once a child is an adult and married or living with someone he (she) will find nothing wrong with having a lover on the side. As a matter of fact, he will encourage his partner explicitly or tacitly to do the same. The early programming pattern says it's the *norm*. If one of the spouses, however, comes from a traditional one-man-one-woman type of family, there will of course be a serious problem. If both partners come from promiscuous backgrounds, the couple may partner-swap forever.

Seeing Parents Infrequently

Let's take the situation in which a girl is left alone a great deal, specifically by her father. He may be a traveling salesman, a merchant seaman, or perhaps he just takes off alone once in a while from his family. Yet in each instance, the father comes back after a short time and is a good, loving parent.

This too, sets a pattern in the child's brain. In later life she expects her husband or lover to "leave and come back." If he doesn't, she will not understand that he loves her. She will then create situations in which *she* has to leave for a while (and in her mind will return).

Eventually, these sorts of situations lead to divorce, unless the husband, too, was programmed to be left alone by his mother. In such a situation, the couple should coordinate the times when their need to be alone is strongest for each of them and things may actually work out well in their relationship.

Love-Imposing . . . and Seymour

Here is a typical example of "Love-Imposing":

"You *must* love me. I expect you to do the things, all the time, that *show* that you love me." Parents often make their child feel guilty if the child doesn't do the things that show love for the parents. It is then not a pleasure for the child to love its parents; it becomes an *unpleasant duty*. In later life the child will feel guilty in its relationships with spouse and friends.

"My mother made me right-handed because I was left-handed. But I am sure that she would have made me left-handed if I had been right-handed." This is how Seymour Weintraub, M.D., in a nutshell, describes his mother. He also explains, "There was an automatic *no!* to everything. She was overprotective and overfed me. She was imposing her love by telling me what to do and how to do it and when to do it and when not to do it. If I did something that she had told me to do, she immediately afterwards asked me 'Why did you do it?' My mother often talked me into being sick so she could take care of me. She straightened out my fingers and straightened out my toes because they weren't straight enough. Mother wanted me to worry about her all the time. She continuously 'suffered' attacks or fainting spells, high blood pressure and imagined heart failure. I am 38 now and still not married. My mother has effectively broken my spirit. Things in my life were always meaningless. I was never accepted as myself. I am still afraid of people and I feel constantly belittled. Our family was Jewish, very orthodox . . . I think we passed religion but flunked life . . ."

Parents Who Don't Keep Promises

Early programming is influenced heavily by the following interaction with parents:

Step 1. I want something from my father (or mother).
Step 2. He promises that I will get it.
Step 3. I wait, I wait, I wait . . .
Step 4. He does not keep his promise.
Step 5. That hurts.
Step 6. I cannot and dare not express my hurt.
Step 7. I cannot trust my father (mother).

The effect in later life: This adult projects that he (she) cannot trust any man or woman who promises something, because no person can be trusted to keep a promise. He doesn't keep promises either. A promise *not* kept has become the *norm* in his life. If a husband keeps his promise to his "doesn't-keep-promises" wife, she will be disappointed that he kept his word. He will soon learn not to promise anything anymore. (Depending on the circumstances, reverse husband with wife.)

The *Then-and-Now* principle is so important in fully understanding the make-up and origins of the hang-up that I will continue to give some more case examples.

Fighting

The programming is as follows: Father and mother are fighting, verbally, physically or both. If their child sees and hears a lot of shouting, yelling, and beating in its home, it becomes part of the child's *norm*. The chip in his (her) computer brain will say, "Home Sweet Home Is a Home with Loud Arguments." Arguments begin sounding like music to the child's ears.

Once married, he (she) will start an argument, any argument. The "fighting"-programmed adult knows his spouse is in love if they are able to happily argue together. If the spouse, however, comes from a quiet home, the opposite is the norm: "A Quiet Home Spells Love."

Either partner may get fed up with that situation and start divorce proceedings. This results in another marriage that is ruined for no good reason and some innocent, beautiful little children become the real victims again. Of course, if both partners come from a loud, argumentative home, they'll have a ball fighting with each other. The whole neighborhood may wish the couple would do something about it. Everyone predicts, if not murder, eventually, divorce. But instead, this couple will actually live happily-forever and ever arguing to their heart's content. They are nourishing each other's survival systems just perfectly.

The Tomboy and the Sissy

When parents have a little girl and proceed to make a little boy out of her or encourage her to be "one of the boys," she'll be a *"Boy"* for the rest of her life. And likewise, the young boy treated as a little girl is going to have many characteristics of a *"Girl"* in his adult life, if his parents encouraged this behavior when he was small.

Religion . . . and Eve

"Eve," said mother, "I want you to know that sex is *sin*. And not only sin, sex is so awful that you'll have to burn in hell and once you get there, you'll never get out."

This was one of Mrs. Johnson's typical conversation with her daughter Eve, from the age of three until she was a young adult. The Johnson family was very religious and they belonged to a Sex-is-Sin Church. Two years after Eve was born, Mrs. Johnson gave birth to another baby. That baby died. Because of this tragedy, Mrs. Johnson had mentally collapsed. Sex had produced her baby and sex was sin. She "knew" that God had punished her personally by taking that baby away. That was her reasoning. Eve, of course, was impressed too. She was there when the baby died. All mother talked about—to Eve, to the neighbors, and to visitors—was the death of babies and the sins of sex. When Eve came to see me in my practice, she was a divorcee.

She had been married for fifteen years. She and her husband had wanted children but the marriage remained childless. He had assumed all along that it was his shortcomings that failed to produce offspring. After the divorce, I found out that he went to see a medical specialist and it appeared that there was physically nothing wrong with him. That put the "blame" on Eve. During her therapy, it became clear that the tremendous forces of fear, as manifested in "Sex-Is-Sin" and even more so in "a baby spells death," did not allow her to become pregnant.

Projection, Rationalization and Misdirection

I will now explain how negative core programming manifests and protects itself. Negative core programming is protected and nourished by projection and rationalization. It works like this:

> **Core programming** Father repeatedly criticizes Harry. Harry in turn feels anger toward his father.
>
> **Behavior in adult life** Harry meets Mr. Jones. Harry *projects* his own thoughts onto Mr. Jones and "knows" that Mr. Jones is going to be critical of him. So Harry is ready to be angry with Mr. Jones before Mr. Jones even has a chance to talk to Harry. Poor Mr. Jones has an angry Harry on his hands and doesn't even know why. Mr. Jones, of course, is totally unaware of Harry's hang-up and the projection that it involves. But since Harry *is* angry (according to Mr. Jones, without reason), Mr. Jones becomes irritated and then criticizes Harry for his uncalled-for anger. And that's all Harry "wanted." But did he really want it? No, of course not.
>
> **Core programming** Julie loves her father. Father does not allow her to love him because he is a cold person. Her love is inhibited.
>
> **Behavior in adult life** Ronald loves Julie. Julie wants to love Ronald but is "not allowed" to. Therefore, she projects and rationalizes that Ronald doesn't love her. Julie is afraid of love. Does she really want love with fear? No, of course not.

These are some of the typical mechanisms of a hang-up. They produce guilt feelings, inadequacies, fears, alcoholism, and in the extreme, murder or suicide. If the problems inherent in a hang-up are directed toward one person, this is called projection and rationalization. We have seen this in the case of Harry and Julie. If the nourishment of a hang-up is directed, however, toward a non-person entity, it is a *Misdirection* of energies and emotions. Some of these misdirections manifest themselves as follows:

Misdirected love   may be observed among religious fanatics and perverted pet lovers.

Misdirected aggression   may be seen among automobile drivers and fanatic spectator sports enthusiasts.

Misdirected sex   manifests itself, among other ways, through philandering, nymphomania, or professional flirts who have sex with many different partners. Includes fetishists (persons who have sex with things, idols, or images), and necrophiliacs (persons who like to copulate with a corpse).

Misdirected endeavor and competition   a work energy that may show up as a status-seeking, image-building and over-indulgence in work. It can manifest itself through neglect of family life, alcoholism and heart disease.

Misdirected intelligence   may be found among heads of criminal syndicates, power hungry politicians, and within the psychiatric/psychologic community.

Warning # I: Hang-ups are habit-forming and are hazardous to your happiness.

The Second-Time-Around Syndrome

A hilarious comedy . . . or is it?

Every night after the dishes were done, Richard and Shirley enjoyed watching television. The couple would sit together, relaxed in their comfortable love seat and looked forward to an evening of peace and entertainment, which they would have gotten if it hadn't been for the fact that Shirley was programmed to *"need"* verbal arguments. Without these fights, there was no love in the family, at least not as far as she was concerned. Her mother and her father had always quarreled. Richard however, came from a *peaceful* family.

During the most exciting part of the movie, Shirley got up, but made sure that she did not disturb her husband. She left the room and returned a few moments later with a can of beer. She sat down and made herself ready to cuddle up against Richard. Richard suddenly pushed her back, got up and shouted "How many times do I have to tell you that I hate it when you leave in the middle of a program? For heaven's sake, can't you wait until the commercial comes? And I am going to tell you something, Shirley, this will be the last time you do this!" He then stormed out.

"What the hell. Why does she have to make me angry all the time?" the husband asks the nice, attractive, understanding female companion who has kept him company during his unhappy periods. Richard shakes his head, turns to her again and says in a low, desperate voice: "You know, honey, my wife doesn't understand me." "I know, darling," she whispers back to him. "Let's go to my place and have another drink."

Unfortunately, Richard and Shirley had never heard about programming and the SpeyerMethods. But now, let's play the same scene again, only this time they know their own and the other one's programming and had gone through the SpeyerMethods.

Same Scene with Knowledge of Programming

Every night, after the dishes were done, Richard and Shirley enjoyed watching television. The couple would sit together, relaxed, in their comfortable love seat and looked forward to an evening of peace and entertainment. Just before an exciting scene in the movie was to unfold, a do-it-yourself wife-warning card popped out of Richard's brain. He read it and said: "Shirley, honey, it's time for your argument. Why don't you get a beer from the fridge?" She smiled at him and replied, "There is no more need, darling. It's all over. No more arguments for us."

They cuddled up together. It was peace and entertainment.

Because they took the trouble to analyze their unhappy behavioral patterns, they were able to identify recurring negative trends, figure out where they came from and then were equipped to take positive action to resolve them. This is what is meant by SpeyerMethods.

Another Scene, Different Setting, but . . .

Tom is an automobile mechanic. He is essentially very good with cars. Yet he loses jobs faster than he can get new ones. In the beginning, all his bosses like him and praise the quality of his work. Sooner or later, however, they let him go because of the stupid mistakes he would regularly make.

Tom grew up with a father who was a perfectionist. He criticized his son endlessly. Nothing Tom ever did was good enough. Tom's bad father-program read, "If you want the love, respect and attention of your father, all you have to do is be sure to do things *wrong* so father has something to criticize." And doing things wrong means making mistakes. *Making mistakes,* therefore, translates into receiving the *"love of your father."* Doing things right, getting praise, was *not* part of his programming. It actually spelled *anti-love*, or in survival language, "death."

Same Scene with Knowledge of Programming:

When Tom started to work in his new job, he handed his brain-warning card over to his boss who looked at it and said, with the utmost understanding, "I bet you can't do anything right, you stupid so and so!"

Tom smiled and knew that he was going to be very happy here.

The human mind is so complex yet operates so simply that it is hard to comprehend. The phenomenon of programming proves this. If it was so *then*, before the age of 3½, it is so *now* in adult life. In order to understand the simplicity of the working of the brain we must first find the *core* experiences. These experiences manifest themselves in a variety of ways, such as: Child does not sense love of parents, child is afraid of parents. Such core experiences are the basis of every hang-up. No more, no less. Each individual, however, projects, rationalizes, misdirects, and wears its own symbols, and expresses not-to-be-fulfilled wishes in his own way. But underneath it all, the influences of the core experiences are the same for everyone.

How to Keep Your Child off the Couch

How do you, dear reader, prevent passing on your hang-ups to your child now that you know about how early programming problems occur? What do you do to ensure your child a happy, well-adjusted childhood and adult life? Or, if you don't have any serious hang-ups yourself, how do you prevent your child from picking up his or her own hang-ups? What are you doing for your child right at this moment? Parents (and prospective parents), here are some of the things you should do:

Basic principle   Since you don't know what your child's future will hold, you must give your youngster strength. Your child must learn from you to be strong in order to be able to cope with any of life's circumstances, both the good and the bad. How do you give your child that strength?

Rule one   Love your child and make it feel secure your love will always be there. You must *tell* the child that you love him (her).

And the child must sense and feel your love. You must be sincere in your feelings toward your child and always sincere when you talk to him. Touch your child. Cuddle your child. Kiss your child and encourage your child to love you, too.

If you don't do all these things, your child will grow up to be an emotional wreck in his (her) later life. And it will have been *your fault*, not the child's. Just as your hang-ups were your parent's fault.

Rule two Your child must have **security**. And if you don't assure this to be the case, the child will be an emotional drifter all its grown life. And again, this will be *your fault*, not the child's, but the child will be stuck with the problem.

Many parents feel that if they are providing food and shelter, they are good and loving parents. They are unaware that their child has emotional needs, too. Therefore, if you give material things only, you are a defective parent and are creating a future wreck, another generation messed up.

Rule three You must **teach** your child the generally accepted moral, ethical and cultural values of the society in which you live. He (she) must learn these values in order to be able to live happily within that same society and within the limits of its laws. If you are negligent in teaching your child these values, it won't be able to accept the law and will end up, at best, in jail. Of course, from the child's philosophical point of view he or she can be an activist or freedom fighter. He can fight against the establishment, but not as a substitute for fighting his parents.

Rule four You have to be **honest** with your child, honest to the extreme. If you feel lousy one day, it's better to tell your child, "Don't bug me. I've got a headache," rather than being angry without giving an explanation. Now the child knows that he is being bugged because you feel lousy and *not* because he has been naughty. You should certainly make it a point to apologize later.

Always be honest in your attitudes. Explain things, don't just do. If you don't explain these things to your child, you will be setting the stage for him or her to grow up to be a liar. You will then find yourself observing the grown-up child lying because you yourself taught him or her this behavior. You will have created another person who can neither trust others or himself. And this end result will be entirely *your fault*, not the child's. Thanks to you, he's gotten another hang-up.

Rule five You have to give your child all possible **freedom** to express himself or herself, verbally and physically. You must let the child play and fantasize freely. However, you must also set the limits of this freedom as dictated by the society, culture and law. This very freedom will give him (her) the opportunity in later life to explore beyond all boundaries, if he or she is so inclined.

Rule six   When you let the child express itself to you and to its world, listen to him and understand. **Communicate.** To express is a two-way street, as is communication. If you don't let your child express itself, you have created a person who is full of fears, has no contact, feels lonely and can't communicate. You have created another tragic individual who will live his one-time life in misery. And it's *your fault*, not his. *But he will be stuck with it!*

However, if you apply all these attitudes about love, communication, security, values, honesty and freedom in a healthy and commonsense manner, your child will have received from you the *strength* to cope with whatever comes along in his or her life. You will have given him (her) the elements to build his *own-person* life.

Chapter Two

THE CURE LIES IN THE "KILL"
or
CEREMONIAL DETRAUMATIZATION: A DO-IT-YOURSELF RITUAL TO GET RID OF ANY HANG-UP

Speyermethods® (SpM) I and II

Research and Correction of Malfunctional Behavior

For Speyermethods® I and II,

First: Heed the Warnings

Warning #2: It is very important that one is self-motivated* to do the SpeyerMethod and is in good physical health. A person with a long history of illness(es) should not attempt to do the SpeyerMethod, despite his/her present motivation and good health.
(*The opposite is denial and/or rationalization.)

Warning #3: Don't do the SpeyerMethod if you are:
1. Pregnant
2. Still nursing your baby (breast or bottle)
3. Under a physician's care (for any reason)—Discuss first with your M.D. or D.D.S.
4. On medication (any)—Discuss first with your M.D. or D.D.S.

5. A frequent visitor (over a number of years) to a psychiatrist, psychologist, psychotherapist or any psychiatric institution
6. On drugs (any) (See note on page 37)
7. An alcoholic (active) (See note on page 37)
8. Related in the first or second degree to anyone who is or was mentally ill
9. Susceptible to suicidal moods
10. If you were involved in a serious accident (of any kind) less than one year ago (see explanation on page 32, Note to Step 2.)
11. If you suffered from a very serious illness (and possibly had an operation) less than one year ago (same as #10)
12. *And if you are in doubt . . . don't do it!*

SpeyerMethod I

The following exercise works as an entirely independent method to accomplish detraumatization. No other exercises or therapies are needed.

Step 1. **Write** Take a sheet of paper (white only, without lines, designs, watermarks or perforations) and write on it (in black only) the name of the person who is currently causing you problems. Make the letters large.

Step 2. **Look** Look at the name you just wrote down. Let this name enter your brain through your eyes and, at the same time, feel sensations or reactions of anger, repulsion, revenge, fear, guilt, etc.

Also at the same time, say or scream out loud these emotions. Take your time to really get in touch with these feelings.

Important: Do *not* continue with Step 3 unless you feel these emotions (Read carefully: "Note referring to step 2" on page 32, in the special instructions.)

Step 3. **Tear** Tear the name you just wrote down and looked at into a "million" pieces. Shred the paper with your fingers (or teeth, if that feels better) and, at the same time, feel the sensation of "killing" that problem person. Let him or her have it! For now and forever! And while you're doing all this, you must talk or shout out loud your hostile and angry feelings toward that problem person.

Step 4.　**Burn**　Put the shreds of paper on a flat ashtray or on any plain white plate (no designs to distract) and burn them. Use a lot of matches but absolutely *no* lighter. While looking at the flames, express out loud your angry feelings. [Be aware of any smoke alarms.]

　　Very important: When working with children, skip the burning! Go directly from "Tear" 3 to Step 5. "Rub."

Step 5.　**Rub**　Take the ashes—all paper must have been burned completely black—and put them in a place where you can step on them, rubbing the ash into the earth* with your foot. Use sole or heel—whatever feels best. This symbolizes that this problem person will never be alive again. Continue rubbing the ashes into the ground until you are satisfied that this person is absolutely *"dead"* and buried in the ground.

After finishing steps 1 through 5, divert your thoughts from the "ritual." Go out of the house or watch TV, do some work, drive your car. Whatever you do, be mentally and physically active. And *don't* think about what just happened. It will be easier for your brain to do the digestion all by itself.

Special Instructions

- If the SpeyerMethod is to be followed, you must, of course, be sincerely motivated to do something about your problem. The SpeyerMethod will not produce the desired effect if it is used as a game or if it is used only as an experiment.
- *No interruption* is allowed. Steps 1 through 5 must be performed, one after the other, without stopping. No telephone calls or answering the doorbell. Do nothing that distracts attention from the ritual.
- *Language:* If English is not your mother tongue, speak your anger, etc., out loud in your native language learned when you were young, age 0–3½ years.

---

*Use the earth in your garden; a tray filled with earth like a litter box; if you have no garden, shred a newspaper on the floor and rub the ashes on top of it; or use a high-pile doormat. If nothing else is available, throw the ashes in the toilet, flush and watch the ashes swirl down into the drain. In all cases, make the rubbing movements with your foot.

- Do the SpeyerMethod on your own, but if you have difficulty getting started, ask a trusted person to help you to get started for your first time.
- You must do the exercise on a *daily* basis, and continue doing it until you have lost all your aggressive feelings altogether. But be aware, that after you think you have lost all your aggression, it is possible you will experience feelings of anger again, a couple of days later. If this happens, go back to the SpM. It usually takes between eight and ten consecutive days.
- You must continue the exercises until *you* feel that they have become redundant. Stopping after one, two or three days may cause feelings of depression and/or nasty dreams.

Special Note for Hypo- and Hyperactive People

Hyperactive Those people who are by nature and continuously overactive—hyper—may experience a depressive or tired feeling after the 8th, 9th or 10th day. This tiredness will rapidly disappear, at which point the SpeyerMethod should be continued until its "natural" end. For hyperactive people this usually takes more than the usual 8 to 10 sessions. This group is especially hyperactive during the Spring and Summer seasons.

Hypoactive Those people who are by nature and continuously underactive—lethargic—may experience a depressive or tired feeling after the 3rd, 4th or 5th day. This tiredness will rapidly disappear, at which point the SpeyerMethod should be discontinued. It may be continued, at a later date, after several weeks or even months, but only if there is still a need for it. This group is especially hypoactive during the Fall and Winter seasons.

(See also notes on Hypo- and Hyperactivity on page 74.)

Note Referring to Step 2

If no feelings of anger come at all, then say out loud the name of the problem person, listening carefully to your own voice, and then try starting all over again. If you still don't experience any feelings of anger, then your problems are too deeply embedded and the SpeyerMethod does not work for you.

This may be due to an encapsulated or otherwise latent illness. Or, it may be due to some other kind of deeply entrenched or latent trauma. Because of these possible circumstances, you may feel incapable or too inhibited to lose your resistance. Consequently, you are unable to react to the SpeyerMethod. Loss of resistance could trigger the illness or trauma to become active. (This is the main reason for *Warning #2* and *Warning #3*, items 10 and 11, both on pages 29–30.)

Basic Principles

The basic principles underlying the SpeyerMethod are the following:

1. Like a computer our brain works with only two basic elements. Computer language is based on 1 and 0 which is equal to the brain's language of Life (which is analogous to 1) and Death (which is analogous to 0). Both elements may also be expressed in human language as "to love" (life or 1) and "to kill" (death or 0).

2. Every man and woman who has an emotional problem with a male automatically reverts that problem (in that person's "computer brain") back to his or her father. Likewise, every man and woman who has an emotional problem with a woman automatically reverts that problem back to his or her mother. This is why when you start to tear-and-burn your problem person, you must always repeat the ritual immediately thereafter with the parent of the same gender as the problem person. In other words, you begin with the problem person of "today" and *always end* with your own father and/or your own mother. If there is no problem person, you may start with your father and/or mother, if they are the main culprits in your life.

3. By combining 1 and 2, you will find the *only* way to rid yourself of these kinds of hang-up problems. In your fantasy, in your brain, the original source (parent) of your problem *must* be "killed," regardless of whether this parent is, in reality, dead or alive. We are not interested in the "good" sides of the parent because their good parenting is not what has created your problems. The object is to isolate bad memories caused by one or both of your parents—and to "kill" these culprits, once and for all.

> *Warning #4:* In spite of all the above-mentioned information, *do not* get involved with analyzing the "technical" details of this method. Don't discuss the pros and cons with so-called experts. Discussions will kill your desire and heighten your fear of ever starting. Don't think. Just *do!*

> *Warning #5:* It is a good idea to do the SpeyerMethod for the first time together with a trusted (nonprofessional) person. Some people find it too difficult to start out alone. Let someone help you take the first step. After the first day the rest will appear to go automatically. Afterwards, *you* help someone you know to take their first step at the SpeyerMethod.

Examples

Here are some examples of the above-described SpeyerMethod. Most examples follow this template:

(A1) Woman with a problem man:

| first do | ⟶ | immediately thereafter do |

| Harry | ⟶ | Father | (or Dad or Daddy, or by whatever other name you called your father when you were little)

(A2) Woman with a problem woman:

| Helen | ⟶ | Mother | (or Mom, etc. see above)

(A3) Man with a problem man:

| Harry | ⟶ | Father | (see above)

(A4) Man with a problem woman:

| Helen | ⟶ | Mother | (see above)

(B) Men and women who lack self-esteem (a more recent, kinder name for the old, so-called "inferiority complex"): Follow the 5-step procedure but, in this case, only with *Father* and *Mother*, one or both. They, together or individually, are responsible for having taken away your confidence which was present in you when you were born.

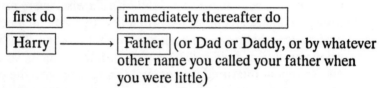

| Lack of self-esteem* | ⟶ | Father | ... and/or ... | Mother |

(C) You can even use the SpeyerMethod if you don't like your own name. Just write your name on a piece of paper, follow steps 1 through

---

*Use your own word best describing that feeling.

5 and lo and behold, you may find yourself starting to like your name, after a while.

| Your own name | $\longrightarrow$ | Father | ... and/or ... | Mother |

(D) If you have any other emotional or annoying problem such as the balding of your head or feelings of inferiority because your breasts are too big or too small, then you can use the SpeyerMethod as follows:

| Balding[1] | or | Breast Size[1] | $\longrightarrow$ | Father | ... and/or ... | Mother |

Note: To be sure, your baldness will *not* disappear and the size of your breasts will *not* change. What does change, however, will be your feelings about this condition.

(E) If you have a problem disliking certain foods or beverages, you can also use the SpeyerMethod to resolve them:

| Fish[1] | or | Milk[1] | $\longrightarrow$ | Father | ... and/or ... | Mother |

(F) You will discover that through the use of SpeyerMethod, some fears can be controlled and sometimes made to disappear altogether:

| Fear (general)[2] | $\longrightarrow$ | Father | ... and/or ... | Mother |
| Fear (dreams)[3] | | | | |

| FEAR (talking) |

Use the word best describing your fear of talking. If you have a stuttering problem that resulted from fear of your parents not allowing you to speak or if they used physical force (e.g. hand on mouth or slap on face) then the SpeyerMethod will eliminate that fear). (See also exercises #11 and #12 on pages 64 and 65).

---

[1]Use your own words to best describe your particular problem.

[2]Use your own word to best describe your fear: E.g. crowds, water, flying, war, holocaust, fire, streets.

[3]Use word describing best the main element of the dream. If you suffer from frightening dreams or repetitive nightmares, these can be completely eliminated by using this method. In this case one needs to first identify one word that summarizes the main element of the dream such as: Shark, snake, wild animal, fire, skeleton, falling, drowning, ghost(s) or any other type of unreal, frightening person or thing— or just a plain scary or nauseating feeling. Not included here are dreams created by fear of *Father, Mother,* siblings, dentists, doctors, etc. For these type of dreams use "Fear" general, above. (See also page 111 for dreams finding their origin in the birth process).

Note: Stuttering that is due to a motor dysfunction of the brain, i.e. information of the right and left brain coming together at the same time at the vocal cords, is not curable through the SpeyerMethod.

(G)   Sexual problems can also be treated with the SpeyerMethod:
Woman: In the event that her problem is frigidity:

$$\boxed{\text{Frigid}^{(4)}} \longrightarrow \boxed{\text{Father}^{(5)}}$$

Man: In the event that his problem is impotence:

$$\boxed{\text{Impotent}^{(4)}} \longrightarrow \boxed{\text{Mother}^{(5)}}$$

(H)   Pain, as a symptom of a mental problem, either diminishes or disappears altogether after using the SpeyerMethod. First you write down the exact type of symptom you are suffering from: For instance, a stomach ache, difficulty in breathing, skin irritation, muscle tension, hay fever, etc. Use your own word best describing the symptom. Then follow steps 1 through 5.

$$\boxed{\text{Pain}} \longrightarrow \boxed{\text{Father}} \longrightarrow \boxed{\text{Mother}} \text{ or Dad, or Mom}$$

Very important warning: If, after 1 or 2 times of doing this, these symptoms do not diminish or disappear, in other words if these symptoms *cannot* be manipulated with this method, (meaning with the influence of your own brain) then the symptom (pain) is *not* related to a hang-up but is pathological (medical) and you should see a medical doctor to treat your ailment.

General Information about the SpeyerMethod

• Sometimes this method works only with one parent. Try both first, but if, after a while, one doesn't produce aggressive feelings, go on with only the other.
• The relationship between the "child" (now an adult) and parents usually improves considerably as a result of using this method.
• If, after a couple of days of trying, the SpeyerMethod doesn't work—or if it does work but produces no real results—then you *must stop!* It may be that your body is signaling for whatever reason that it does not want to give up its resistance.

---

[4]Use the best word that relates to your particular problem: fear, pain, no excitement.
[5]Father is "men" in later life; mother is "women" in later life. For homosexuals, do the parent of the same sex.

• Although in most cases this method will be over in 8 to 10 consecutive days, there are some people who need additional time. This is particularly true of those who are still confronted, on a daily or frequent basis, with that "you know who" problem person. In those cases it may take longer to produce the desired effect.

To resolve your conflicts relating to a continuous confrontation situation, you must possess an adequate amount of will (survival) power. If you happen to be a little short of it, get a friend with good common-sense qualities to help you see the light. "Confrontation situations" usually happen under the following circumstances:

1. Still living at home with your parents.
2. Seeing your boss at work, every day.
3. In spite of trying, you can't seem to break with your lover or, of course, with your ex-lover, or ex-mate.
4. If you are still in transference to a psychiatrist/psychologist or any other type of counselor, etc., or to an organization such as a cult, be it religious or secular.

If you are already in the process of attempting to rehabilitate yourself, you may even try the SpeyerMethod as an additional tool for dealing with problems related to:

Smoking │ or │ Drinking │ or │ Gambling │

or │ Drugs │ or even on │ Cancer* │

No need for ⟶ │ Father │ or ⟶ │ Mother │ unless they caused your problem.

After you have finished the entire SpeyerMethod cycle and are convinced that you have reached a satisfactory end, go to page 49 and carefully read the chapter, "After the sessions are over."

Advantages

No cost† – *no* appointments – *no* transference – *no* medication – *no* drugs – an almost immediate result – and it can be taken as easily as an aspirin for a headache!

---

*Consult your doctor first!
†Except for the price of this book.

SpeyerMethod® II

" . . . to 'kill' a hang-up"

SpeyerMethod II is designed to be performed between a motivated person who wants to get rid of his hang-ups and a trusted nonprofessional friend or acquaintance willing to help him. We will refer to this person as the "Helper." The focus of this chapter is the helper. The hung-up person will be referred to as the "Subject."

If after the subject has done SpeyerMethod I, there is still a need to go more deeply into the problem, I will teach you, the helper, how to get really to the heart of the matter. Do you remember our Survival System #3 on page 4? Well, now we are going to work with those primitive signals, Life and Death. In our method, as stated before, Life equals Love and Death equals Kill. Here we do not use Life and Death but instead we are going to work with Love and Kill. This is the only language the brain speaks when it comes to combating a hang-up. You must understand that we are now going to work with absolute core elements of human life, the basic building blocks. They can be interpreted, dressed up, or symbolized as follows:

Love is: to love – to like – to be kind – to feel sympathy, friendship, warmth – to understand – to hope – to congratulate. In other words, we have a wardrobe of words all fitting the core-body **Love** (Life).

Kill is: to kill – to hate – to dislike – to be unkind – to be irritated – to be angry – to harass – to compete – to curse. All, in the final analysis, mean **Kill** (Death).

All of the following exercises are based on the "kill-or-love" principle

---

The culprits who created the subject's hang-up, his or her negative computer programming, are in "99 out of 100" cases the father and/or mother. But whoever else was instrumental should also be considered the culprit.

In SpeyerMethod II we are going to eliminate the parent's bad attitudes from your subject's brain. And we are going to do that by using your subject's fantasy. In his (her) fantasy he has to "kill" his parents. I want to emphasize again that the word "kill" is used in the same sense as when a little child uses it when he wants his parents "dead," because he doesn't get his wish, for instance, an ice cream.

"Kill" is the most primitive expression to get someone who stands between a person and his desired object out of the way. The "kill" concept is found in the expressions of every language. In English, for example, it is found in the phrase "Drop dead."

Instructions, Warnings and Important Observations
Relevant for SpeyerMethods I and II and all exercises

SpeyerMethod II should be done between two people, one willing to help and one willing to be helped. So come along with me and listen to the swan song of your hang-ups. But first, let me give you a couple of warnings:

Warning #6: Before anything else, the subject must see his physician and explain what he intends to do. Let the doctor read—or buy—this book and if there are no objections you may start. *Note:* This warning is for the subject's protection because some of his symptoms may have a medical basis.

Warning #7: The SpeyerMethod must be carried out with the true welfare of the subject in mind. If the helper and/or his subject start out to work the following procedures with malicious thoughts, with expectations of new mysterious experiences, or just for the fun of it, these SpeyerMethods won't work. The helper and his subject have to be sincere, honest and interested in doing something about the subject's problem.

"For Whom These Words Toll"

1. For those people who are strong willed and strongly motivated—who want to grab their own problem by the horns—and who want to do something about them, on their own.
2. For those people who know other people who walk aimlessly through life, seemingly never to succeed. Or, if they begin to succeed, will run away from success. They can then act as a "Helper" with these hung-up people. The "Helper" may be a good friend, a relative, a colleague, etc. The person acting as the helper must draw the attention of the hung-up person to the SpeyerMethods, as described in this book. Then, the helper

must make the subject start with the SpeyerMethod and help him or her to complete the entire 5 step cycle. In the event the subject doesn't mind and if there are two people willing to act as helpers, this is permitted, too.

3. Pressure groups: They could be relatives, peers, colleagues, friends, clergy, executives, bosses, teachers, doctors, family members (even children), club members, students, clients, judges, etc. These people—one or all in concert—should pressure the "sufferer" into doing the SpeyerMethods, offering to be the helper or even helpers (see item 2, above).

4. Peer and executive pressure in the workplace.

   Some employees and some executives within a corporation, institution, governmental agency, etc. will be trained at a SpeyerMethod facility to become a helper (available in Europe and soon-to-be available in the United States). Once a person goes through the SpeyerMethod he himself can act as a SpeyerMethods helper to others. Eventually, every employee/executive will be able to avail him(her)self of these SpeyerMethods, in their own workplace.

5. For socially minded volunteers such as: Retirees, senior citizens, people temporarily unemployed, part-time workers, religious organization members, labor union members, nurses, teachers, students, single parents, husbands and/or wives, etc.

   Eventually, it will be ideal if there is at least one person available as a helper, on every block of every street, in every town and city. Every "sufferer" could then walk in without an appointment set up long in advance costing exorbitant sums of money, and be helped in a matter of minutes. If this is the case, nobody in the hung-up person's environment need know about it. The price to be paid to the helper should never exceed the price of this book. Helping people get over their problems does not have to remain the lucrative, money-making endeavor it has been turned into by many of today's profit-oriented health-care professionals, and as it is, with very limited results, anyhow.

6. How to find that trusted helper? Sometimes you will discover you can tell your deepest secrets to a total stranger, someone you meet by chance on a train or plane. Or at a bar, beauty parlor, hotel lobby or park bench. What gave you that gut feeling to tell your personal story to a total stranger? Why did you trust that one particular person and not another person? In order to find that trusted person, who will eventually become your helper, you have to simply go with your gut feelings. It

works as well as any other method, even better! After the SpeyerMethod has been completed, your helper will become a friend for life.

7. How do you—the sufferer—ask a trusted friend or an acquaintance to help you do the SpeyerMethods together? Let him or her read this book and, while discussing it, suggest that you would like to do the SpeyerMethod with him or her. That is the easiest, most direct way to get started.

---

8. Now, you—the ex-sufferer—are ready to become a helper to some other needy person, someone you know will benefit from your experience.

"If someone—in his grief—tells you: "There is no God and all people are wicked," go and stand next to him and say: "But I am here!" This is an old Hassidic saying.

General Exercises

The purpose of the following exercises is to let your subject actually come to the point—in his (her) fantasy—that he wants to kill his father and later on his mother, or even his sisters and brothers or any other culprit who may have contributed to his hang-up.

In order to get the subject to this point, he has to say out loud the names of his parents, just the way he used to call them when he was small. The sound (wave frequency) of the subject's utterance of the word "Dad" (or Papa or Daddy or Father) or "Mom" (or Mama or Mother) goes back into his (her) brain. There, these words will search out and activate the subject's memories of his parents as experienced in his early childhood years. Through mentioning a person's "father-call" or "mother-call" one can find among the billions of brain cells, those particular circuits holding the memory of "Father" and "Mother."

The helper's aim must be to inspire the subject to get rid of his anger toward his parents—and later toward the other culprits—by actively participating in the process. In other words, you must encourage the subject to perform "the kill."

Initially, one subject may find it difficult to let go while another may start the "killing" process spontaneously. But as long as the subject— with your help—repeats his "Father" or "Mother" call, memories and reactions to these memories *will* come. And when they come, he will express them by being angry at his parents. The subject's anger should leave his brain through his muscles: Fingers . . . fists . . . hands . . . arms . . . jaw (biting) . . . legs . . . feet . . . shoulders . . . back. And also via his vocal cords: Shout . . . scream. Sometimes all this "killing-of-the-parent" is preceded by, sometimes followed by, or sometimes mixed in with, crying.

As a helper, your attitude both before and after the active sessions must be one of understanding, kindness and warmth. Yet, at the same time, you have to be a benevolent authority figure as well.

During the actual sessions, however, you must be in complete command and control of your subject. He or she has to follow your orders and instructions. You literally have to pull him along on that road toward the "kill" of the culprits. That road has many obstacles and it is your determination, your commanding voice, and your instructions which eventually will get the subject there. "Being nice" doesn't help here much. As a matter of fact, it is a hindrance.

After your subject has had some outbursts and has to rest, you should be sweet to him (her), praising him and saying, "We're doing just fine." Caress the subject's hair or cheeks, or pat him on the back. However, as soon as the rest period is over, your tone of voice must again be instructive and commanding.

Warning #8:

1. Work as mechanically as you can.
2. Control your own feelings and excitement.
3. Be aware especially of your own feelings, be they anger, fear, sexual excitement or disgust.
4. Don't be carried away by your own feelings because you will then not be able to accomplish what you have set out to do.

Read the following instructions *very carefully* before you start to work with your subject.

The following steps have to be taken (and they should be rehearsed a couple of times before you start the actual sessions):

First, a list of the necessary materials: Bed, chair (no armrests), firm pillow, paper tissues, sleeping mask, towel.

The Start of SpeyerMethod II

1. Your subject is fully clothed.
2. He must remove his contact lenses or glasses.
3. His mouth must be empty. No food, chewing gum, etc. Dentures are allowed.
4. (She) must not wear make-up.
5. He must take off his shoes.
6. He must not wear any jewelry around his neck, wrist, fingers, or (her) waist or ankles.
7. No tight-fitting belt around the waist or any tight-fitting clothes are allowed.
8. Tell your subject to sit on the edge of the bed, about half-way between the two ends.
9. Tell him to close his eyes.
10. He must be fully aware that his eyelids are closed.
11. Put a tissue over his closed eyes.
12. Cover the tissue with the sleeping mask.
13. Then lay the subject down on the bed (from his sitting position). Put one hand behind his head—as in holding a baby—using your other hand to guide his legs onto the bed.
14. Find the right spot as close as possible to the edge of the bed, but give the subject room enough to have his arms lying next to his body.
15. The subject is now on the bed as close as possible to you.
16. You sit on a chair, next to the bed.
17. You face your subject.
18. Your position must be between his shoulders and his hips.

    Note: You will have to be close to the subject when you hold the pillow while he is punching it and also when he whispers and you have to have your ear close to his mouth.
19. You sit on that chair, close to the subject, facing him. Now, put the subject at ease by asking if he feels nervous. If he does, tell him he should feel nervous. It's his first time and something unknown is going to happen to him. But do not go into any discussion with him, ever, at this stage.

    (*Note:* Ask if the subject is comfortable. He must be flat on the bed—no pillow under his head. Move his body until a comfortable spot is found.)
20. Now you tell your subject to relax: "Just *feel* yourself on the bed."

21. Continue: "Breathe in deeply—hold your breath . . . tighten your muscles . . . breathe *out* and *relax* your muscles."
22. Breathe *in*, tighten muscles . . . breathe *out*, relax muscles. Muscles to be tightened are, face, jaw, shoulder, biceps, fists, buttocks, legs, toes, stomach. (Repeat 21 and 22 three times, then proceed to 23.)
23. Tell your subject to relax his brain: "Drain your brain, drain all the thoughts and tensions . . . and *relax.*" (Repeat this 3 times.)

Make a couple of dry runs before you start

The Kill-or-Love Fantasy Story

After you finish relaxing your subject, tell him the following fantasy story:

"In your fantasy you are looking at a measuring stick that runs from 0 to 100. The midpoint '50' is clearly marked. The '0' is on the left and the '100' is on the right.

The '0' on the extreme left, is called kill.

The '100' on the extreme right is called love.

The midpoint is '50' the neutral zone, where kill changes to love.

The reading is from left to right.

Start your story by saying to your subject, "Say out loud the name of your father (mother) and listen carefully to the sound of your own voice."

Subject: "Dad . . . Dad . . . Dad . . . Dad," (or whatever other name he used to call his father when he was little). Ask him to tell you at what point on the measuring stick he finds his father (mother) to be.

Helper: "Now, either *kill* or *love* your father (or mother)."

No other choice or hesitation allowed! It's either Kill or Love!

Some subjects may start with seeing only "today's" problems instead of father or mother. They are so overcome by them that in the first instance, those are the ones that come pouring out. Excellent, let them come. Let him first get rid of these surface pressures by letting him react and talk about them. Then, let him relax and start with *"Kill or Love"* all over again.

If nothing happens at all, that's all right too. The purpose of Day One is to let the brain become acquainted with the use of the fantasy system to think backwards in time.

But, when you feel that your subject is ready to go into "killing," you have to coax him to use his muscles and to talk loudly, even to shout.

While he is expressing his anger toward the one parent with such words as, "You are no good," "You never loved me," "You always left me alone," etc., suggest to him that he emphasizes these feelings by banging his fist on the bed. As soon as he does that, stand up from your chair, take the pillow (which you had handy all the time) and put it under his fist, next to his thigh.

Coax him to continue to beat, hit and shout against the parent. He is in the process now of killing. This time, you must inspire your subject to use both arms and fists while expressing his pent-up anger. You must hold the pillow a little above the subject's belly, catching his blows with your pillow.

If he starts to cry, encourage him to cry. At some point he will show signs of getting tired. Tell him to relax and rest for a moment.

Then tell him to breathe *in* deeply and breathe *out* slowly. Let him do that a few times. (It is a good idea to do this breathing exercise yourself with him.) Ask him (her) to look at the measuring stick and to tell you at which point—number—he is at now. Ask your subject this after each outburst.

Then, let him start all over again. When the beating on the pillow gets too rough to handle for the helper, instruct the subject to relax. If he does not react right away, take off his mask and tissue and order him to look around. He will calm down immediately.

After a little rest period, put the tissue and mask back on and continue giving him the choice between *killing* or *loving* his father (mother).

> *Warning #9*: At all times, the subject must hear his helper's *voice*. The sound of the helper's voice is the only communication the subject has with *reality*. *This verbal contact must be maintained at all times, regardless of how many sessions are to follow!*

In the next phase the actual "killing-in-fantasy" is going to take place. The subject must "kill" his parent with whatever muscles he chooses. He may use his fists or flat hands to hit his father (the pillow), his feet to kick, his jaw to bite or his hands to strangle his father's neck (in which case, you give your subject the towel). In his fantasy he may *not* use a gun or poison, not use karate or similar chops, or concoct a scheme to kill his father (mother). These types of killings have been learned *after* his programming years (0 to 3½). To be effective, we have to keep it biologically simple.

The reason that one subject uses his hands and another one his feet is that during the programming years the brain has sent instruction to "kill" to specific muscles.

Those are the ones the subject elects to use automatically because the pathways between the brain and the muscles are genetically determined.

Once the subject has started SpeyerMethod II *he must go on!* It will take an average of eight to ten sessions, one a day, of about 30 minutes each. The subject must go on until *he* determines that his parent is *"dead."* And you can be assured that he will know when. He will let you know by saying so, *or* he may say, "I still want to kill him." In that case, more aggression is waiting to come out. You then continue with *"kill* or *love"* until the subject starts expressing some measure of *"love"* for his parents. In the beginning, this may be just a forgiving, "Well, I can take him now," or "Well, I can understand him now," or "I am still afraid to love him." Then ask your subject again at what point on the measuring stick he is (remember he is still blindfolded on the bed). Once the subject has crossed the midpoint '50' mark, he may go all the way to love his parents, but he doesn't necessarily have to. Just over '50' is good enough. Most subjects find that their greatest problem is to get from just before the '50' mark to just after.

The Sounds of Papa and Mama

Very Important!!! While the subject is in the "killing" act and says out loud his father's or mother's name, the helper must continuously say, *"Go On!"* However, the helper must also tell the subject *"Say Father"* (using the name for father your subject is using) when your subject does *not* say his father's or mother's name aloud.

The words the helper uses to encourage and coax his subject toward the "kill," as well as during the "killing" process itself, must be repetitions of the subject's own words. For instance, when the participant calls his mother a "bitch," say the same word aloud but only as a repetition and as an immediate follow-up after the subject has said it. In other words, support your subject with the identical words he or she uses.

When the subject is silent, *you* keep saying, "Say the name of your father (mother) out loud and listen to your own voice, say Dad (Ma)"—if that's what he called his father (mother)—"and listen to your own voice."

After a rest period, switch back and forth between "father" and "mother" like this: First you say "father" and let the subject do all the shouting, fighting, and reacting. Then give him a little rest. Next switch to "mother." Then rest and back to "father." Rest. And so on.

If there were any sisters, brothers, grandparents, other relatives, or strangers like a neighbor or the doctor, use their names as well to determine if the subject has any negative feelings about them too. If so, include them in the "killing."

Keep an eye on the clock and see to it that these sessions do not last longer than 20 to 30 minutes. In cases, however, where there is a complete violent reaction you must go on until the subject is tired out. You will notice that the subject will indicate more or less when the session is over for that day. But *you* must be the judge of whether to stop or go on.

Aiming

One very important item is that the helper has to direct his subject's aggression and/or his sadness to the source from which it originally came, the parent. In other words, your subject is *never* allowed to be simply angry, just using any word or only expressing anger through his muscles. The subject *must always* focus that anger and mention the name of the parent he or she is fighting or is sad about. If he doesn't, it is your very important task to make him do so by instructing him to "Say father," or "Say mother." And while he is "killing," he *must* continually talk to that particular parent.

This is what I call "aiming." It is important for the helper to know that, if he doesn't aim his subject's anger/sadness at the *original source*, he can go on forever and the SpeyerMethod will not produce any permanent results. If the subject aims at the defective parent, then after a number of days, the subject's aggression, anger, and sadness reservoir will be emptied out.

Down to Zero Test

To test if *all* aggression and sadness have really gone, the following three exercises are necessary.

1. When your subject finally expresses some form of love or understanding for his or her parent(s), put the pillow on top of his chest, (the subject is blindfolded on the bed) put his arms around the pillow and instruct him to express out loud love for his father (mother). While the subject is in the middle of doing so, you—with a sudden jerk—pull away the pillow from under his arms. At the *very same time* you jump in with the words: "Kill or Love."

   Because of the shock, your subject will feel the aggression all over again and will start to do some more "killing." Keep repeating this until he doesn't mind the pulling away of the pillow and it has become meaningless to him. At that point, leave the pillow on his chest, with his arms around it and let him express, if not love, some positive feelings toward his parent(s). *You* remain *silent.* Your subject will end the session.

   [Sometimes these talks are very emotional and dramatic and you yourself may get tears in your eyes. Don't be ashamed of your own feelings. Make sure, however, that your subject doesn't see this—that he *is* securely blindfolded.]

2. You say, "Say the name of your father (mother) out loud and listen to your own voice." Your subject calls repeatedly the name of his parent and you repeat after him the same name as he utters it—also out loud. Like so: *Subject:* "Dad!" *You:* "Dad." Do this five or six times and tell your subject: "Let this name *vibrate* through your brain."

   Then say, "In your fantasy, each of your feelings and emotions are like tiny dots on a square screen. Now, you're going to scan the screen from left to right, from top to bottom. Say out loud the name of your father (mother), if any of these dots light up— meaning you still have a negative feeling—express this to me." If the subject does, repeat "Kill or Love" again until there are no more reactions on the screen.

3. This time *you*, the helper, say the name of the subject's parent out loud. While you do that the subject *listens. You* observe every muscle on his body: Feet, legs, fingers, hands, arms, shoulders, stomach, face, lips. If, upon the sound of "Father" or "Mother" any of the subject's muscles makes a movement, tell your subject what's happening with his muscle(s) and proceed to let him do more "Kill or Love" and test again and again until there are no more muscle movements.

When you read all this for the first time, it sounds difficult to do. But I guarantee you that eventually, after a couple of dry runs, it becomes routine.

After the Sessions are Over

Hosanna . . . but not yet.

Warning #10: There will be a three months digestion/adaptation period

---

After you finish each session—your subject is now sitting on the edge of the bed, his eyes closed, a little dazed—put your arms around his shoulders, put his head on your shoulder, and tell him to relax. Wipe the subject's forehead if he is sweating, comfort him and ask, "How do you feel?" Tell the subject that you are going to take off the eye mask. Remove it carefully. See to it that his eyes are opened slowly. Do not let too much light get into the eyes too suddenly. Kiss or pat the subject gently (on the cheek or forehead, as you would kiss a child who has just hurt his finger). You are the *good* "parent" now. Let the subject linger on your shoulder until *he* has had enough pampering. Sometimes, at this point, your subject may start crying. Let him cry and comfort him.

At the end of the period of solace, ask the subject whether he feels tired and drained *or* nervous and tense. If he is drained, it means that his brain has completed its "killing" cycle for that day. If he feels nervous, it means that the cycle has not been completed. In this case, you have to warn your subject that he may feel depressed between now and tomorrow. But tell him not to worry and tell him to phone you if he needs to or feels like talking to someone.

As a result of having done SpeyerMethod II your subject will go through some personality changes. Since many obstacles and inhibitions have been removed, a freer person emerges.

Digestion Period

It is very important to realize that some changes have taken place in your subject's mind and body. He is bound to have reactions. These short-term reactions manifest themselves as a depressive feeling, or may be acted out in some form of childhood protest, or may manifest themselves as a need to reject everyone and everything.

In most cases, such reactions are directed towards the subject's immediate family and relatives, his friends and even in the workplace. As a matter of fact, these reactions have to come. And when they do, you may congratulate yourself. They are *the indicator of success*.

The reaction period may vary from day-to-day during the first two weeks after the last session and sporadically thereafter, while working itself out over a period of three months. A *low* point, which may include a period of "old" problems again, may also be expected during the second month after the last session. This low point will last from a couple of hours to two days at the most.

During the first two weeks after the sessions, the subject's feelings will alternate between "good" and "bad," although in the beginning of this period, bad feelings will occur more frequently than good ones. Between the tenth day and two weeks after the last session, the subject will reach a low which will last from a few hours to a maximum of two days. This low will manifest itself as a depressive feeling.

The entire digestion period may be off schedule because of bad circumstances in your subject's daily life. Such circumstances could include financial difficulties or generally unpleasant situations. In these cases, your subject might mentally collapse and the depression will come sooner.

The reaction may also be postponed because of outside pressures on your subject's daily life, such as a pending exam, or having to finish a project with a tight deadline.

Physical illness, known or unknown to your subject, will also move the low point in either direction, regulated by the strength or weakness of his resistance. During the first couple of weeks after the end of the sessions, it often seems as if the SpeyerMethod did not help at all. The subject will have strong doubts and fears because he may feel worse than before. His state of mind *has* to be that way and it means that you are on the right track.

During the SpeyerMethod digestion period the subject's brain is putting in order all newly experienced information and is actually fighting against its "old" self.

After these first two weeks are over, until about five weeks after the end of the SpeyerMethod, the subject will feel good and bad in turn, but this time the good feelings will prevail. The subject may experience these good feelings with amazement or disbelief.

After this relatively good time, the digestion period will end with a convulsive and desperate last grasp, as the subject tries to hold on to his "old" self. He will reach this low point about six weeks after the last session.

At this point, he will start to feel lousy again. Shortly after that, the subject is going to be in really bad shape. He will be depressed and feel the SpeyerMethod didn't work. The subject's family, relatives and friends, job and the whole world will be felt to be no good. In short, the subject will reject everyone and everything. Although the prelude to this rejection period may last several days, the actual low will vary from a few hours to a few days.

Adaptation Period

From here on, the subject will be entering into his *adaptation period*, also lasting about six weeks. He will want to turn away from all the old "hang-up" situations to which he felt attracted previously. Now the subject will experience them as superfluous, even irritating. He will go out and find new situations in life which belong to his real self, and not as before, to his old hang-ups.

Sometimes it may happen that during or even after the three month reaction wave, a void develops. The "old" self has gone. The "new" one hasn't arrived yet. The one thing the SpeyerMethod has no control over are the sets of circumstances in your subject's life.

During that void, one may revert back to a religious feeling similar to that which was prevailing within the family when one grew up. In such case, it may happen that one becomes a born-again Christian, an Orthodox Jew, seeks temporary retreat in a monastery, or joins a religious or semi-religious cult. If the hold of the institution is strong and the participant is weak by nature, the subject may have found happiness. When this weakness has been reversed back to strength he will, sooner or later, come back "into the real world."

Note: All the above-mentioned time periods are based on averages. Dates and low and high points may therefore vary slightly, but not much.

Warning #11: Do not make any *important* decisions during this three month digestion/adaptation period. *Your feelings will change continually during this period.*

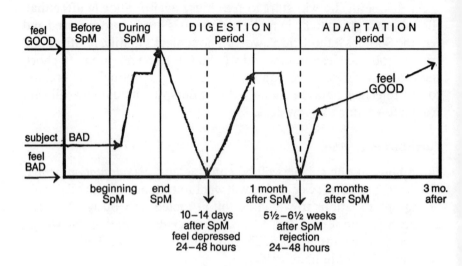

feel GOOD	Before SpM	During SpM	DIGESTION period	ADAPTATION period

Time chart

An Afterthought . . . That Should Have Come First

It's so comfortable to sit in my easy chair and say. "It's all caused by faulty programming." What pain does a person really feel all his life, trying to do the right thing, and never succeeding? Even if the subject and I together are to succeed and shake out the bad old hang-ups, how can the subject make up for those lost 20, 30, sometimes 50 years of pain, struggle and unhappiness? The answer is of course, that he *can't!* Those years are lost forever. What a truth . . . What a tragedy . . . What a *curse* . . . .

To rear a child does put an enormous amount of responsibility on the shoulders of the parents. They are the ones who can create a life full of misery for another human being, the very human being that was born out of them. If couples intend to become parents and they have no sincere intentions to do right, to do good, to love their yet-to-be-born child, they should not conceive a child in the first place.

Before the wife becomes pregnant, she and the husband must know the consequences of child rearing. They must *want* the child and *know* even before conception, that they will love their child.

Long before conception, husband and wife must discuss whether or not they want children. They should tell each other how, separately as well as together as parents, they are going to treat their child. Before creating that child, it is all-important to be aware of what actually is going to happen within that family in the future.

> *Rule Number One:* You must love your child *before* it is conceived.

This should be a *law* and we may as well add it to the second amendment to the fifth Commandment: "Honor your father and mother but only if they loved you before you were conceived."

Chapter Three

IF IT HURTS . . . FIX IT

Mind over Body

The basis for "Hang-up Problems Accompanied by Physical Pain" is formed during the period from just before birth until about 18 months of age.

During this period a baby lives in an animal world of instincts. He (or she) has a physical mind. He can express himself only through and with his body. He can't talk yet, can't symbolize. He can only signal. The baby has the need to be held and to be touched. To feel his mother is how he understands his mother. He has to sense that she is there only for him. Her touch, her tone of voice are primarily the only communication the baby has with his mother. The mother must understand that her baby's touch and sound is his only language.

If the baby feels only the body warmth of his mother but does not sense love and sincerity, he will express his unhappiness, actual fears, and insecurity through his body.

What else could possibly make a baby feel unhappy? ("Unhappy" being a kind word for fearful and life-threatened.) It can be caused by not feeling secure in his mother's arms or in his crib. His mother can either overfeed him or not feed him enough. His mother can also be impatient during the feeding.

The important thing underlying all those inadequacies, however, is the misunderstanding between mother and baby. The most devastating thing to the baby is not sensing the love of his mother. In order for these unhappy situations to develop into physical problems in later life, they must have continually prevailed for at least six out of the first eighteen months. When a mother has had an occasional bad day, it will certainly not influence the child's happiness in later life.

When the baby feels the need to express himself in order to change miserable conditions and situations, he will shout out his unhappiness both vocally and through his body language. His body really doesn't want to expend electricity (energy) but if it has to, it will follow the road of least resistance (as all electricity does). Unhappiness, therefore, will be expressed through the weakest (genetically weakest) part of the baby's body. An unhappy baby with a weak stomach will become colicky. The very same baby with a strong stomach but a weak respiratory system will develop breathing difficulties instead, from simple coughing to asthma.

Some other indications of expressing unhappiness are: Rashes, allergies, overweight, underweight, hayfever, hives, inflammation of the eyes, sinus trouble, and more. If your baby has any of these physical problems and you are a good mother, you will see your physician. The above mentioned manifestations of infant unhappiness may carry over into adulthood. For example, a colicky baby may develop ulcers in later life.

The following vicious cycle of events is the basis of all physical problems caused by insufficient love and security in very early childhood.

Step 1. Baby loves mother.
Step 2. Baby doesn't sense mother's love.
Step 3. Baby is unhappy.
Step 4. Body expresses baby's unhappiness.
Step 5. Baby becomes ill.
Step 6. Illness damages body.
Step 7. Damage causes pain.
Step 8. Physical pain makes baby even more unhappy.

We have now the beginning of an almost never-ending interaction of mind over body. At the adult level, the unhappy "adult baby," sensing without conscious awareness an unhappy situation, will tend to repeat the same physical expression as he used when he was an infant.

Sometimes, when we are very young (0 to 18 mo.), the brain sends instructions to certain muscles to perform a certain function. If, for one reason or another, these brain-to-muscle instructions are not carried out, this electricity (instructions equal electricity) will remain "sitting" in that particular muscle. Its influence might be felt, for instance as a spasm, for the rest of one's life.

It is, however, possible that these brain-to-muscle instructions are forwarded and deposited in one or another organ, preferably the weakest in the body. This can lead to serious illness in later life.

But these no-love situations can continue after 18 months, too.

Case in Point: Dennis

"My father loved my brother more than me." This was the main complaint of Dennis, age 35. However, this very attitude of his father seemed at the same time his good fortune. "My brother Ed, who is about 40 now," said Dennis, "has become an anti-social neurotic. I remember that Dad was particularly cruel to Ed. He got all the love but all the beatings, too."

Dennis came to see me because he had suffered from muscle spasms in his back ever since the age of 5. He had seen a number of medical specialists but the spasms continued.

During the therapy it became obvious that there was a strong identification with brother Ed. Because of his father's love for Ed, Dennis wished that everything that had happened to his brother had happened to him, too, and the identification had to include the beatings and the pain as well.

He actually felt his brother's pain every time he saw Ed being hit by their father. At one point, Dennis witnessed his father, who was building a do-it-yourself storage room, hit his brother with a two-by-four. Dennis "wished" at that moment, that *he* had been the one to be hit. He made an automatic protective move by pulling up his shoulder muscles against the expected blow. It was his brother that got hit, but Dennis' brain had sent the necessary electricity (instructions) to his shoulder and his back muscles to tighten for protection and to catch that blow. The blow he "wanted" so much never came. The electricity in the muscle was never released.

On the therapy bed in my office Dennis was relaxing, lying down on his stomach, eyes closed. I told him to visualize that same picture again: His father starting to hit Ed with the two-by-four.

"When I count to three," I instructed Dennis, "you must feel—in your fantasy—that blow coming and hitting your shoulders and back." At the count of three, I tapped him with a flat ruler across his shoulder blades. He went immediately into a spasm which worked itself out in a few moments. Dennis described it: "It rolled away like an orgasm." (It is indeed the same principle.) The tied-up electricity in his muscles was released. He finally got the "Hit of Love" he had been waiting for for almost thirty years.

Geraldine and Alice

Geraldine is 23. Ever since she started to menstruate at age 13, she has had almost unbearable premenstrual pain. Over the past ten years, she had been examined and treated by many well-known medical specialists. Nonetheless, the monthly pain continued. Therapy produced the following traumatic memory:

At age 3, Geraldine witnessed, by accident, her mother miscarrying. The miscarriage happened unexpectedly on the toilet in the bathroom, just as little Geraldine walked in. She saw the blood running from her mother's vagina and down her legs. That was all she saw and Geraldine thought that her mother was dying.

Such a scene is a tremendous shock for a girl that age. This traumatic experience became the basis for her premenstrual trouble. Every month, just before she had to menstruate, she subconsciously "thought" that she was going to die. She therefore tightened her muscles, thus preventing the blood from running out. Holding up the blood flow was painful. Once the flow finally started, the pain stopped. After re-living this traumatic situation in SpeyerTherapy, the menstrual pain stopped.

Alice is 23. Ever since she became a "woman" at age 13, she had had constant pains in her rectum. During the past ten years or so, she had been examined by many well-known medical specialists. The pains continued, especially when she was excited or under stress.

Therapy produced the following traumatic memory:

At age 3, she was taken horseback riding by a young man. They were riding bareback on the same horse, she in front of him. Because of the movements of their galloping horse, he held her with his left arm around her waist, his left hand pressing down on the lower right side of her abdomen. Alice bounced up and down on the horse's back. Alice's father was a cold, unaffectionate and distant man. He never touched his daughter. According to Alice, the young man on the horse was a real macho-man. For the first time in her life she met with and felt masculinity. (To a girl this age, this is an actual sexually exciting feeling.) With these emotional as well as sexually exciting feelings came, at the same time, the pain of bouncing on the horse's bare back and of the young man's cramping hand on her abdomen. After realization and some exercises, both pains disappeared.

To all Geraldines, Alices, and Whoever:

If only one of the many medical practitioners, specialists, internists, or gynecologists they went to had considered a possible mental trauma–related basis for their pain, years of needless suffering could have been prevented.

Orphans of the Medical Profession

I feel very justified in my criticism of the medical profession because too much needless suffering is going on. Believe me, Geraldine and

Alice were two of the "fortunate" ones. Others needlessly end up on the operating table or suffer for a lifetime. If a pain continues after a thorough medical investigation and treatment, do not forget to take into consideration the possibility of mental trauma–related causes. Forgetting this has happened too often, causing unnecessary suffering, the beginning of another hang-up, and the loss of one's quality of life.

The medical profession is treating mental trauma–related symptoms as "orphan children." They really don't know what to do with them. They are so used to prescribing pills, tablets, and capsules that they are unable to understand, and often unwilling to understand, that some of these symptoms should *not* be treated with medication.

SpeyerTherapy and SpeyerMethods I and II are so simple that they alarm the medical profession, often only because of their simplicity. Regardless of the welfare of their patients, doctors refuse to accept them. Later in this chapter, I shall tell you how simple they are and—what's even less liked by the profession—how anyone can do them.

Overcoming a "Painful" Problem

Again, this SpeyerMethod, too, can be done between two people, one willing to help (the helper) and the other one willing to be helped (the subject). As a matter of fact, it is so simple that almost anyone can help another person who happens to have this sort of *hurt* hang-up. But first, let me give you a couple of (repeat) warnings:

Repeat warning #6 Before anything else, see your physician. Some symptoms may have a real medical base. (Read the entire warning on page 39.)

Repeat warning #7 The SpeyerMethod must be carried out with the true welfare of the subject in mind. (Read the entire warning on page 39.)

Heed the warnings #2 and #3 on page 29 then *follow exactly the instructions, warnings and observations on pages 41 to 44* including *steps #1 through #23*

Introduction

The Purpose of the Exercises   The purpose of the following "touch" exercises is to release stress, tension, or spasm, all equaling excess electricity, from our body system. This "releasing" will happen through evaporation, explosion or convulsion from those muscles and organs, including one's voice and tears, which hold programmed infant and childhood instructions yet to be activated.

The Use of the "Helping Hand"   By putting your (the helper's) hand on one particular spot on the subject's body, specific traumatic memories relating to that particular spot on the body will come back, thereby releasing the stored electricity in the muscle or organ that causes the pain. (The actual exercises start on page 61.) Helpers can be sure that good and pleasant memories will come back, too, but these are not what we are interested in. The good and pleasant memories have not created the problems. Therefore, you are always after the negative reactions such as: Memories of fears, hurt, pain tension-situations, loneliness, punishment, confinement, intimidation, terror, horror, panic, fire, war, Holocaust, etc. When touching your subject on the specific places on his or her body as hereafter taught and shown, you must be prepared for a reaction from that muscle or organ.

Muscle: The subject will use this muscle *now* the way he intended to use it when he was little, *then*, but never did!

Organ: The subject will feel pain or discomfort as a reaction to your touch.

Muscle and Organ: The subject will push away your touching hand. After each push you should bring back your hand to the same spot, time and time again, until your subject reaches that moment in which he realizes it is *your* hand and that pain or irritation has stopped coming back. From that moment on your (helper's) hand feels "sort of good."

Do this over short periods of time—30 minutes at the most—but repeat it the next day again until the pain or the discomfort doesn't come back at all—and at this point do it just one more time. You have to come to a point where your touch becomes totally meaningless to your subject. This goes for all touch spots. The exception is when, from the first time on, your touch feels "sort of good" to your subject. You don't have to continue touching that spot after a few times of "feeling good."

At other spots, however, the subject may start to fight rather than push away your hand. In order to cope with that situation you must use your pillow to catch his punches. Under these circumstances, do not remain sitting on your chair. Stand up. This will be easier for you because by standing you have better control of the situation.

When you observe that your subject is getting tired or exhausted, let him rest and breathe in deeply three times. That will bring his energy back for the next battle.

If you are afraid you will lose control, tell your subject to stop, relax, and take off his mask. Then, start all over again.

Repeat warning #9 At all times the subject must hear the helper's voice. It's the subject's only communication with reality. (Read the complete warning on page 45)

The Actual Exercises

First, follow the instructions on page 43, steps 1 through 23. Then, tell your subject this: "I am going to touch you on several spots on your body. As soon as you feel the touch, you are going to tell me what you feel. Every square inch of your skin has a representative in your brain and the two are connected. So, every time I touch you it will give you a memory of what happened to that particular square of your skin. Let me give you an example. Do you have a scar anywhere on your body?"

Your subject indicates a certain spot on his body where he has a scar. *You* put the tip of your finger on the scar and say: "Feel the touch on your scar and tell me the first thing that comes to your mind."

The subject will explain how he got the scar. He will say, "When I was five years old I fell through a glass panel and cut my right hand."

You would then reply, "This particular spot reminds you of that accident. Now I am going to put my finger on another spot of your body."

This time the helper places the tip of his finger on another spot on the subject's body, a few inches from the "glass" scar and says: "Feel the touch and tell me the first thing that comes to your mind." The subject will think for a long time but won't come up with anything. Then you (the helper) say: "Whatever you feel now (on the second spot), this touch did not bring memories of the glass incident, did it?"

You have now demonstrated to your subject that some parts of his body, when touched, bring back certain memories related to that particular area of the skin.

If your subject does not have a scar, or has a scar on an impossible place, put your finger on the spot where he ordinarily wears a ring or a watch. When the scar is underneath his clothing, put your finger on top of his clothing, pushing slightly down on the scar. Make sure it is the exact spot. Let your subject guide you until he is sure.

Of Utmost Importance!!

How can you discover if a pain or an uncomfortable feeling is indeed related to an infant or childhood trauma or if it is real physical pain?

Warning #12 The answer lies in being able to *manipulate* the pain or the uncomfortable feeling.

If the pain *disappears* upon the helper's suggestion or with exercises, then the origin is related to a hang-up.

If the pain *can not* be manipulated, it is pathological (medical). The pain will remain no matter what the helper does.

You, the helper, are now going to learn how your subject will react to touching. On some spots he may have severe reactions, on some others very little and on others, nothing at all.

You start by saying: "OK . . . first spot," and touch spot #1 (see below). In all subsequent touches, announce *in advance* that you are going to touch your subject and what specific part you are going to touch. For instance: "Now I am going to put my hand on your left biceps." Never surprise your subject.

At or after the touch, look for reactions. Do this at all spots from #1 to #23. And remember your goal: *"Kill" the culprit!*

- Your subject is and remains fully clothed, at all times.
- In all the following cases, the subject has to push away the helper's hand or pillow.

1. Put your hand around his right biceps

Touch lightly and say: "Say the first thing that comes to your mind." Let the subject's verbal and/or physical reactions follow. Depending on the intensity of the reaction hold your hand around his biceps a little tighter or move your hand up and down, pulling his biceps up and down.

Some common reactions from the subject are usually: Memory of father or mother or other persons pulling him somewhere against his will. Encourage the subject to fight off this feeling until he feels that it is your (the helper's) hand and he doesn't react any longer to your grip or pull. If there is no reaction at all and the touch doesn't bother him or even feels good, go to the next spot. But check it out thoroughly. This goes for all subsequent spots. Keep announcing in advance where you are going to put your hand or finger next.

2. Put your hand around his left biceps

Touch lightly and say: "Say the first thing that comes to your mind." Then, continue along the same procedure for 1 above.

3. Put both your hands at the same time around both the subject's biceps, left and right

Touch lightly and say: "Say the first thing that comes to your mind." First just touch, then push him down on the bed, but do it gently. It is the touch that brings back the early memories, *not* the strength. As a matter of fact, if you push too strongly, you may actually cause some real pain which will get your subject out of his childhood memories and into today, and you don't want that to happen.

If he reacts to your light touch, let him have his full fling. Be sure to use the pillow and let him call out loud the name of the parent or other person associated with this particular touch. If he is tired, let him rest and instruct him to breathe in deeply. Then resume the same touch until he feels *your* hand and no longer the culprit who started it all.

Always tell the subject to continue to react until he recognizes *your* hand instead of the original culprit. Always put an *end* in front of him. Like so: "Go on, until you know that it is *my* hand."

4. Put your hand on his right shoulder

Touch lightly and say: "Say the first thing that comes to your mind." First lay your hand lightly on his shoulder and wait for reactions. Then push his shoulder a little more firmly down on the bed.

5. Put your hand on his left shoulder

(Same procedure as for #4.)

6. Put both your hands at the same time on both shoulders

Shoulder reactions often have to do with school or other fights which the subject lost by being held down. Sometimes the reaction is a feeling of helplessness. Sometimes he just wants to let go of his feelings. In that case, let him push away his "helplessness." Whatever word he uses, you use.

7. Put your hand gently around his throat

Put your hand as low as possible around his throat, barely touching. Rest your hand on top of his collar bones.

The subject's reactions will usually have something to do with suffocation, other breathing problems, strangulation, etc. Sometimes his reactions may be symbolic, such as pressure from parents. But whatever it is, let him fight. On this and all following throat touches, let him breathe in deeply after each reaction seems to be finished. Then continue.

8. Put your hand gently around his throat

This time in the middle. Rest the middle of your palm on his Adam's apple. The rest is the same as for #7 above.

9. Put your hand gently around his throat

Now on the upper area, touching the bottom of his jaw bone.

10. Put the tops of your spread fingers vertically on his throat

Use your four fingers, *not* the thumb. Your four fingers should run vertically from the chin down to the spot where both collar bones meet. Don't be afraid of near-suffocating actions made by your subject. If he didn't suffocate *then*, in his childhood, which he obviously didn't, he will not suffocate *now*. He is just repeating the same movements that are still stuck in his throat from his childhood time. He may make vomiting gestures. If this should be the case, try to get your subject to vomit. Have a pail ready, a glass of water, a towel, and for your as well as for his sake, some fresh-smelling wet towels.

11. Put your hand on his mouth

Place it over his mouth, in half-moon fashion, barely touching his lips. Remove your hand and put it back again. Repeat this frequently.

A typical symbolic reaction: He is not allowed to talk. Let him push away your hand and start all over again his fight to "kill" his parent.

12. Put your index finger across his lips

Again, this in half-moon fashion barely touching the lips. Lift your finger and put it back on his lips. Do this frequently. Typical reactions have to do with a "filthy" taste, such as Grandpa's kiss and the taste and smell of tobacco and alcohol. Let him fight it off.

13. Put the top of your index finger on the middle part of his closed lips

Tell him in advance to close his lips. Barely touch the lips with your finger. Be aware of the fact that he may, all of a sudden, bite your finger! Lift your finger from his closed lips and put it back. Repeat this several times.

Typical reactions are: A wanted or an unwanted kiss, a penis is his/her mouth, the doctor's ah-stick (spatula), someone's finger. Whatever reaction comes, let him fight the negative memory and get it out of his system.

14. Touch both his eyes

Touch both eyes *very gently* with your thumb and the top of your index finger of the same hand, at the same time.

15. Touch and pull slightly on his right ear

16. Touch and pull slightly on his left ear

Your subject may suffer from supersensitive hearing. He hears everything much more loudly than people with normal hearing. Most of the time, however, he doesn't know that his hearing is supersensitive and blames his surroundings for excess noise. Supersensitive hearing cannot be treated by the SpeyerMethod. Your subject should go and see an ear doctor.

If you discover that your subject has such a problem, you must explain the effects of it on his daily life and within his family unit.

Other reactions will have to do with parents, teachers, siblings, etc. Sometimes an old ear infection will be remembered.

17. Slap his right cheek

Very softly, barely touching.

18. Slap his left cheek

Very softly, barely touching.

19. Lay your hand around his forehead

This may be done quite firmly. Make a half-moon between your stretched thumb and index finger and press down on the subject's forehead. This may produce a headache. Let him push away the headache, your hand. Repeat this till the headache is gone, but be aware that after a short while the headache will return. Keep repeating till the headache doesn't come back any longer.

Note: If he is a regular headache sufferer, disregard this exercise. He should see a doctor before attempting it. Other reactions are: Kept in a "vise" by his parents. Let him free himself by pushing your hand away. Keep repeating until he feels relieved from that vise-like feeling.

20. Put pressure on the top of his head

Put your full hand on the top of his head and push downward in the direction of his feet, first gently, then with more pressure. Typical symbolic reactions: He is held down, made to feel little, or is not allowed to grow. Let him fight and "kill" the culprits who have done this to him.

21. Pull his hair backward

Do this gently, don't hurt him.

22. Put your hand under his neck

Hold your stretched thumb and index finger in a half-moon fashion and lift the back of his neck just a little.

23. Hand on chest bone

Make a fist of your hand. Use the flat side of your fist, that is the area between the lower two sets of finger knuckles. Then put your flat fist on your subject's chest bone and press down slightly. When your subject is a female you should not touch either breast. This will give a different reaction from the one you are looking for.

Exercise 23 is usually a strong symbolic reaction point. Typical: Being held down by parent(s) or fighting one's way out of pressure situations imposed by his parents against his will.

When reactions get too severe, put the pillow on the subject's chest instead of your flat fist, and catch his reactions that way. You may also keep the pillow in the air above the chest to catch his punches.

24. Hand on stomach

Announce: "I am going to put my hand on your stomach. Tell me the first thing that comes to your mind." Then, put the flat palm of your hand on his stomach. Stomach aches or "air bubbles" in the stomach should be treated like all other symptoms. Let him push your hand away until the pain or uncomfortable feeling has disappeared. Here again, if these pains are chronic, he must see a doctor first!

25. Hand on belly (abdomen)

26. Hand on lower belly

Say: "I am going to put my hand on your lower belly." Put your hand above and partly on the pubic hair area and say: "When you get any sexual feelings, just say so. It's perfectly normal to feel that."

27. Put your subject's right hand on his penis (her vagina)

(If you feel awkward about this, then first read the important note on page 90.)

Take your subject's right hand with your hand and put his (her) hand on his penis (her vagina). Hold your hand on top of his (her) hand. If there are any negative, fearful, or painful sexual reactions, put the subject's hand next to the body and use only your own hand to touch the genitals. Typical symbolic reactions: *Male:* Feels castrated—wants to be masculine, but can't. *Female:* Feels guilty and fearful—wants to be feminine, but can't. [For actual physical sex problems, see Chapter Four, page 81.] If the reaction is: "It feels sort of good," continue to

28. Put your subject's left hand on his penis (her vagina)

Put pressure on his/her hand with your hand. Continue with the same procedure as number 27. If there appears to be an actual physical sexual problem, like pain or a very strong fear, turn to Chapter Four for further instructions. In either case, however, symbolic or physical, let your subject push away your hand from his penis (her vagina) until the feeling of inadequacy is gone.

29. Put your flat hand against the inside of the right thigh

First, just gently lay your hand on the spot. Wait for reactions. Then, push your hand with some shock effect a little deeper into the thigh, even to pushing the entire right leg a little.

30. Put your flat hand against the inside of the left thigh

Same as for 29 above.

31. Put, simultaneously, your right and left hands against the left and right thighs

Push thighs away from each other with a jerk. In case a rape memory should surface, turn immediately to page 99 in Chapter Four.

32. For women only: Put her right hand over her left breast

Exert some upward pressure by putting your hand on top of her hand. Ask for reactions. If there are reactions, use only your hand and let her push away your hand until the problem has been "pushed" away altogether.

33. For women only: Touch her left nipple with your index finger

If you can't find it, ask her to help you find it. Look for reactions.

34. For women only: Put her left hand over her right breast

35. For women only: Touch her right nipple with your index finger

(32 through 35) In case of reactions, use your hand or pillow, when necessary. Typical reactions related to the subject's breasts are: Pain or fear when touched, too small, too big, subject feels inferior about her breasts or about her own femininity.

If your subject has had a mastectomy (one or both breasts removed by surgery), let her express her grief, her fears or her feelings of helplessness, if any of these feelings are prevailing.

Tell your subject to switch to his belly

He must change his position from lying on his back to lying on his belly. Help him in doing so.

Check his eye mask. Put your subject on the spot on the bed where you want him.

36. Put your hand around his left buttock

This time you start with his left side because he has turned around. Pull up his buttock with a jerky movement.

37. Put your hand around his right buttock

Same as 36.

38. Put both hands around both buttocks

Let your fingers of each of your hands point towards each other, in the middle between his right and left buttock. Pull buttocks away from each other with a slight jerky movement of your hands.

39. Push your index finger slightly against his anus

Over his clothing, of course, and push a little inward.

Typical reactions are: Mother's nails while cleaning her child's rectum or a rectal thermometer caused some traumatic experience for the child. These traumatic childhood experiences are sometimes a problem for adult homosexuals.

40. Put your hands around his waist

Hold your thumbs on his backside and the rest of your hand on his belly side of the waist. Push hands inside, towards each other. Some people are ticklish. If that is the case, let go and do not pursue.

41. Put both hands on his shoulder blades

Place one hand on each blade. Push upwards in the direction of his shoulders.

42. Put one hand on his spine

Push gently upwards in the direction of his neck. Then, in opposite direction, towards his buttocks.

43. Put your hands around his shoulders

Push down a little.

At this point, announce that you have finished

Miscellaneous messages

Tingling:

Sometimes your subject may get a tingling feeling in his fingers, arms, legs, chest, head or even throughout his entire body. This usually starts when he is still on the bed, but may continue thereafter. It means that there was an excess of electricity in those cells that contained the trauma information. Sometimes this excess electricity is released throughout the body system and appears as a "tingling" sensation.

At first, your subject will be fearful of this sensation. Explain to him that he is losing his hang-up pains in this particular manner and he should be happy with the tingling.

Wait to continue the exercise until the tingling disappears. *Do not* discourage the tingling.

Breathing

To treat certain breathing difficulties the helper must explain to the subject that the windpipe and the bronchial tubes are surrounded by circular muscles. In his fantasy, the subject—who is still blindfolded— must "look at" his own windpipe and tubes. The helper says: "Tighten the muscles around the windpipe and feel a suffocating sensation." Helper waits until the subject indicates he feels just that. Then the helper says: "Relax the muscles around the windpipe and breathe in deeply." Repeat this exercise several times and do it rhythmically, like so: "Tighten muscles (subject must experience breathing as being difficult), two . . . three . . . four. Relax muscles—breathe easy . . . two . . . three . . . four."

When you say, "Tighten muscle," you put your finger or your hand gently on his throat. When you say "relax muscle," remove your hand from the area.

Keep doing this till he has learned this conscious control mechanism and realizes that he *can* control his breathing difficulties with his *brain!*

Touch

In general, to get rid of physical problems related to childhood traumas, all you have to do is put your hand (finger) on the painful, irritating or uncomfortable spot and say to your subject: "Just push the pain away until it's gone. Say out loud, 'Go away pain,' with all your anger and willpower." All your subject has to do is push away and talk or shout away the pain, using all his anger and all his willpower (willpower is survival).

The Helper's Workload

To handle all these touch points seems like an awful lot of work, taking forever. This is not so. Generally speaking, this type of session consumes as much time as any other one because your subject will react only to *some* of these touches, definitely never to all of them. Yet, in some cases it may take so long that you don't finish in time (maximum 30 to 40 minutes). In that case you will have to do the rest of the exercises the next day. Make a note of the number of your last touch point and continue with the next exercise when you resume the SpeyerMethod, tomorrow.

After the Sessions Are Over

Hallelujah . . . but not yet.

Observe all warnings and observations on pages 49 through 52

Body over Mind

Homosexuality, Lesbianism and Bisexuality

Now that we have seen that our brain is the super computer regulating interactions between itself and our muscles and organs in such a simple fashion, nobody will be surprised to find out that this brain of ours regulates *everything* we feel, we do, we think, we make . . . in short everything *we are.*

In my opinion, there is essentially only one base for the phenomena called homosexuality, lesbianism and bisexuality.

A physical origin—an inherited (genetic) hormonal balance which differs from the heterosexual hormonal balance. And, as a result a mental state of mind in one or both parents is prevailing because of that hormonal anomaly. This is often reinforced by one or both parents' attitude toward their child during its crucial programming years.

In More Detail

Physical   Homosexuals and heterosexuals think and behave according to proportions of male and female chromosomes and hormones of the embryo, from which they stem.

Homosexuality may be one symptom of a biological process in which Natural Law reduced childbirths to protect us from overpopulating the world we live in.

The Homosexual Mental State of Mind   When a boy grows up without a father or without any type of male authority around him during his programming years, he does not receive an image of a male in his brain. If this fatherless boy has a domineering mother, who is and acts as a strong authority figure in his life, the boy will be programmed to see a woman (instead of a man) as the authority figure. Because he has no father to imitate, he will imitate his mother. He becomes a "woman" and then nourishes his inherited hormonal balance. The very fact that his mother *is* "manly" and that she has chosen to be without a husband, or has chosen a weak husband, is related to both parents' hormonal make-up.

Some men have only homosexual tendencies. In their programming years, there might have been a father in the house, but he was weak, vague, or did not give a sense of authority to the child. He had submitted his male powers to his strong and domineering wife. Mind you, these types of parents are frequently very happy together. They provide a need for each other. Some of their traits, which they, in turn, inherited from their ancestors, will naturally rub off on their offspring.

Girls who grew up without a father, or with a weak father, but have a strong domineering and authoritative mother, will follow the same pattern. In later life, they are attracted to women who represent to them the "male" authority. But again, a latent homosexuality has to be present.

Another basis for homosexuality is when a boy under the age of 3½ is sexually caressed by his father or by another man. This experience may become a sexual habit in later life. It has been accepted as the norm. The same holds true if a young girl is routinely sexually caressed by her mother or by any other woman.

If this sort of situation starts after age 3½ the boy and the girl will grow up with homosexual tendencies, combining sexual excitement with fear and guilt feelings. They will also be able to have normal sexual relations with members of the opposite sex. They are bisexual. Some bisexuals enjoy this double life to such a degree that they would not have it any other way. They feel sorry for the pure heterosexuals as well as for the pure homosexuals. According to the bisexuals, all others "are missing half the fun."

In heterosexuals the boy loves his mother and wants to "kill" his father (Oedipus), but with homosexuals it's the opposite. He loves his father and wants to "kill" his mother. Homosexual girls (lesbians) love their mother and want to "kill" their father.

Without any doubt, heterosexuality is the general norm at this point in the evolutionary process of the human species. But since homosexuality involves someone's personal happiness, his innermost privacy, no one should ever sit in judgment . . . !

Case Study

Lenny: age 43, famous producer of stage shows and movies.

Family background: Poor, typical ethnic.

Problem: (In Lenny's own words) "All my life I have walked around with the feeling that all men would beat me up and all women would turn me down for another man. I am always afraid. Nobody in the world really ever has cared about me. In spite of my success in my work, I have no confidence in it. As far as women are concerned, I can only enjoy a woman if she doesn't know that I exist. If I have my eye on one and if she doesn't know that I exist, I steal her panties and masturbate with them. I am fascinated by the look of a woman's rear end. I love to kiss it and smell it. Sometimes I do have sex with a woman, but mostly with men."

Life story: "I was born in a very poor family. We lived in the back of Papa's store, all in one room. I slept in the same bed with my parents. I was the most beautiful baby in the family. Mama made me wear dresses and let my hair grow long. When I was in my mother's arms, it felt good. But it never lasted. She immediately put me down again. At that point, I always got such a shock that I thought I would never see her again. That made me very sad."

Note: When Lenny loves a woman, he creates his own situations of sadness in order to make true that he'll never see her again (projection).

"When my father beat me, I ran away and sought refuge under Mama's long skirt. Mama liked me to be under her skirt. Mama and I, we both liked that. At other times, when I was under her skirt, I could see her panties and smell her rear end. Sometimes she abruptly pulled me away from under her skirt and my father continued to beat me. When I was 13, I was afraid of girls. I was scared of guys too. One day, I went to the movies and next to me sat an old man. He started to play with my penis and I came. From that moment on, I knew that I was a homosexual.

"I guess my father noticed my homosexual behavior. One day, he gave me $2 and sent me to a prostitute. I looked at her nude body and left. No sex. The frustration in me was that I was attracted to men but wanted women. I always wanted a woman but ended up with a man."

Hyper- and Hypoactivity

There are mental conditions which have nothing to do with hang-ups and in which the person is perfectly normal, yet his flow of energy is constantly too high or constantly too low. Sometimes it alternates between too high and too low. These expressions of nature are usually inherited. If one's energy is constantly too high, an extremely strong need for expression is apparent. The person is a constant talker, moves his hands and feet, can't sit still, and is generally overactive. He can hardly listen to other people because listening adds energy to his already over-filled brain cells. He can neither properly assimilate nor objectively analyze incoming information. He has to be strongly extroverted and is a go-getter. Persons of this type who happen to have a bad programming as well, and are therefore strongly inhibited, sometimes explode in sudden outbursts, often hysterical. In the sexual domain, some high-energy persons can perform almost "endlessly." Women of this type can climax ten to fifteen times during one session of intercourse.

There are interactions between energy levels (inherited) and inhibition levels (parent programmed). They may manifest themselves as follows:

1. A normal energy level with few inhibitions is normal.
2. A somewhat higher energy level with some stronger inhibitions may cause a person to be active, overactive, expressive, or extroverted, except in his emotional language.
3. A much higher energy level together with a much higher inhibition level may cause a person to exaggerate all the time, even to become hysterical some of the time. However, he can barely express emotions.
4. A super-high energy level with an extremely high inhibition level may cause a person to develop schizophrenic conditions (he may even be a killer) or possibly cancer.

When the energy level is too low, a generally depressed attitude is apparent. The person is lethargic and inactive. This, however, should not be confused with a possible thyroid condition.

There are other cases in which the energy flow alternates between too high and too low. The person is overflowing with happiness one moment, only to fall into sadness the next. These people are labeled as manic-depressives. They are alternatively expressive and depressive. Yet, it's not all that black and white, because people with too high energy levels often fall back, for a short period, into a low energy lull, sort of a breather to recharge again. In this case, they need fuel and listen, for instance, to loud music (= fuel).

Energy levels usually express themselves in four different directions: physical, sexual, emotional, and intellectual. There is usually a combination of two. The one that can prevail by itself is our sex drive. It's called Libido, by some.

Neither homosexuality, bisexuality, lesbianism, nor hypo- or hyperactivity fall into the domain of SpeyerMethods.

But, for those who are constantly overactive, or have a constant feeling of stress, or have an overabundance of energy, or who can't ever seem to be able to relax*:

_Do_[†]	_Don't_[†]
_Do_ sleep in complete darkness	_Don't_ use a sun lamp
_Do_ take a nap during day/evening	_Don't_ take cold showers
_Do_ exercise, and do sports	_Don't_ eat sweets/sugar/honey
_Do_ participate in fitness programs	_Don't_ eat any food with yeast as a base
_Do_ eat lots of citrus fruit, tomatoes, and other high acidity foods	_Don't_ drink alcohol, chocolate, coffee
_Do_ take vitamin C	_Don't_ smoke
_Do_ meditate	_Don't_ take any of the vitamins of the B complex[‡]
_Do_ relaxation exercises	_Don't_ frequent noisy places or listen to loud music
_Do_ take hot bath/shower, sauna, hot tub	_Don't_ use an electric blanket

---

*The emphasis is on constant, practically from day of birth. Or, sometimes only during spring and summer.
[†]In case of illness, deficiencies or minimal brain damage (MBD), M.D.'s advice always has priority.
[‡]or any other yeast based, over the counter vitamins or minerals.

Do have sex as often as possible   *Don't* expose yourself to the sun
or masturbate

For those who are constantly tired, or have a constant feeling of
having insufficient energy, or have a feeling of losing energy*:

Do[†]	*Don't*[†]
Do sleep with the lights on	*Don't* take naps during day/evening
Do use a sun lamp, especially during fall/winter	*Don't* exercise or do sports
Do take a cold shower after waking up	*Don't* participate in fitness programs
Do take a glass of wine each day	*Don't* eat citrus fruits, tomatoes or any other high-acidity foods
Do eat sweets, sugar, honey	*Don't* take vitamin C
Do eat any food with yeast as a base	*Don't* take aspirin
Do take vitamin B complex regularly[‡]	*Don't* meditate
Do frequent noisy places, always listen to radio/Walkman, watch TV	*Don't* take relaxation exercises
Do sleep under an electric blanket, fall/winter	*Don't* take hot bath/shower or sauna/hot tub
Do frequent sunny/warm places/climate	*Don't* have sex if you're not comfortable with it

Health, from Ancient History to Science Fiction

At some time in the future, we will discover that normal health will
turn out to be nothing more or nothing less than the perfect balance
between hydrogen and oxygen, on the atomic and sub-atomic levels,
in each cell in our body (and in all biological life, of course).

---

*Constant—or primarily during fall and winter—because *temporary* tired feelings, as
frequent as they may be, are usually a typical reaction to hyperactivity.
[†]In case of illness or deficiencies, M.D.'s advice always has priority.
[‡]Or any other exotic energy booster, such as Ginseng, Royal Jelly or Co-Enzyme Q 10,
products of Dr. Aslan (Rumania) or Prof. Niehan's cell therapy (Switzerland).

When this perfect balance is distorted or destroyed, illness becomes apparent. (This does not apply directly to illnesses caused by foreign materials, infective agents such as bacilli or viruses, or to damage caused by accidents or injuries.)

Looking far back into the history of the health sciences, we see that some ancient medical practitioners were already using methods of curing illnesses by using the principle of restoration of the perfect balance between hydrogen and oxygen. To name a few:

- Acupuncture: Putting "positive" energy from the atmosphere into sick cells, or, as the need may be, drawing "negative" energy from sick cells and letting it evaporate into the atmosphere.

- Yoga: Through special breathing methods, combined with physical exercises, oxygen is directed to those places in the body where hydrogen (without enough oxygen) would otherwise build up too severe a pressure.

- Meditation: It lowers the hydrogen content of the brain and body cells wherever hydrogen happens to be too high. Unfortunately, however, at the same time it lowers hydrogen in places where it is needed. This, by the way, is the pitfall of deep meditation when it is done over extended periods of time. It then lowers the body's resistance and consequently, its immune system.

- Medical insight of the Pharaohs' physicians: Directing oxygen to a pain area by breathing in deeply and holding one's lungs full of air, while looking, at the same time, with one's "eye of the mind" (closed eyes) at the painful area. This is called "imagery" these days. These sorts of exercises are still practiced today, for instance by the Ancient and Mystical Order Rosae Crusis and similar organizations.

- Lao-Tse's teachings and Taoism reach "the balance" with touch, stroking, breathing and muscle exercises.

Some time in the future we will invent a detector that can scan cells for possible hydrogen/oxygen imbalances. We will then be able to direct the needed element to the proper area, thus bringing a major part of medical science back to the simple methods with which our forefathers operated. As a matter of fact, in the future we will need more medical technicians and fewer medical doctors. At some point in the future, we will have an electronic body scanner, which we can hold in the palm of the hand, showing a digital read-out relating to the degree of health and the degree of illness of every part of our body system. (We already have it in cars!) We will then be able to dial the appropriate code on this little hand computer and it will emit and direct a specific sound frequency to the sick area of the body, in need of "medication."

In other words, all old-fashioned medicines and acids like aspirin and Vitamin C shall have been translated into "sound tracks." Every medicine of today will be a "frequency" tomorrow. No more substances, just waves. They will reach the needed areas "by ear and by skin." Science fiction? I don't think so.

The Sound Works of the Brain

Let me give you a few indications of how sound works. It is used in all SpeyerMethods. One purpose of the phenomenon *"pain"* is that it is accompanied by sound that our body uses to cure. Cells which are lacking electricity (= pain) are filled up again through outcries of pain, vibrating into our body through the ears and the skin. This will put electricity (read: the pain sound) back into the emptied cells. When the pain stops, the outcry (screaming) stops.

In the original SpeyerTherapy, depressive feelings are cleared up with sound. Let me read to you from the SpeyerTherapy instruction manual:

"When the patient seems to be too deep in a depression, turn on your little (handsize-pocket) radio to a station with the loudest possible noise—preferably erratic music. Hold the radio a few seconds against each of your patient's ears, alternating it from right to left. Soon the patient will be out of his depressive feelings. It takes approximately 12 minutes after you stop putting sound in his ears.

"Sound, in this case, is electricity going into the brain, filling up again that which he had lost during catharsis.

"Very important: In this case, sound does not alleviate the actual problem that caused the depression. It only clears the depressive feeling connected with the problem.

"Primitive tribes (and the not-so-primitive discos) use sounds such as drums, cymbals, wailing, shouting and screaming as pain and depression killers." This much from the manual. But there is more.

To cure illnesses like cancer, rheumatism, diabetes or hypertension, when caused by stress, sound waves should be administered through ear and skin while the patient says out loud, or thinks about, or sees in his fantasy, the organ or the growth in its proper location, even though his eyes are closed at all times. (Closed eyes is the switch that lets electricity go out of the body system.)

Future practitioners of medical science will regard the 20th century doctor in just the same way as the 20th century doctor regards the primitive medicine man of deep dark Africa.

After all these sound works, let's go to some more upbeat "therapies" of facial expressions, *smiling, make-up* and *feed-back.*

Smiling

When one smiles, specific face muscles have become automatically active. This is a one-way street going from the brain—where the reason for the smile is located—to the face. When we have no reason to smile and we are depressed but activate the facial "smile" anyhow, it becomes a one-way street too, this time in the opposite direction. We signal the brain that we are "happy." The unhappy or depressive feeling will diminish and one is then better equipped to deal with the negative cause(s).

Make-up

Putting make-up on your face expresses that you feel good about yourself. Or, you put make-up on because you want to feel better about yourself. In either way, you hope that the outside world will take notice of you. So, if you feel lousy one day, put make-up on your face. However, the only way to let it work then is to look at yourself in the mirror and smile . . . see above! The same goes for a man, grooming himself.

Feed-back

You know that some people over 45 (or thereabouts) will lie a little about their age. They usually make themselves a couple of years younger.

However, I suggest that, as of your 45th birthday (or thereabouts), you start having birthdays twice a year. In other words, up your age instead of downing it.

The result will be that people will say: "Gee, you look terrific for your age." And that kind of feed-back should give you an equally terrific feeling, a feeling that will create a smile on your face . . . (see above).

And, if you want to call this lying . . . then, so is lipstick.

Chapter Four

SEX . . . IF IT DOESN'T
WORK . . . FIX IT

Basic Principles

There is too much sadness in human life because of sexual problems accompanied by sheer ignorance. In order to appreciate these writings to the fullest extent, you, the reader, and I, the writer, must have as a point of departure that we will accept sex as an absolute necessity and a normal and pleasurable function of our psyche as well as of our body.

Sex, in all its manifestations, free or inhibited, is a most important part of every person's life, especially when there are problems attached to it.

Common sense tells me that sex problems must be exposed and discussed openly, freely and without shame. Sex influences, to a tremendous extent, our personal as well as our social lives, and indeed cultural, economic, and political life in general, be it either openly or "under cover." Just watch the media or read history, including the Bible, and you'll understand how and why.

If today, for the first time in history, a surgeon were to cut open a human body in order to remove a diseased organ, the world—with its intense communication systems—would actually be physically disgusted by such an act. It would be considered contempt of the highest order for a most sacred taboo. (Another scenario on page 90.)

To rub a woman's vagina, or a man's penis, in order to cure her of frigidity or him of impotence, is still such a sacred taboo today to many. This chapter must, therefore, be read with the realization that a break-through of such a taboo is a disturbance of the human ethical status-quo which will always arouse Man's disapproval of Man. In the long run, however, as it is in the case of the surgeon, this type of method (SpeyerMethod II) will prove to be beneficial to mankind in general and to a satisfying sex life in particular.

A General Insight into Sex Problems

As strange as it may seem, sex is *not* regulated by the penis or vagina, but is regulated, in the first instance, by the eyes, the ears, the sense of smell and the skin (touch) . . . in other words, by the brain. First, one has to be "turned on," but "turned on" holds as a necessary consequence that one can also be turned off. If all this turning on and turning off happens when *you want it,* everything is fine and dandy. But if you start to be turned on and you want it to go all the way and, damn it, against your will your sexual response is turned off—or if you can't get turned on at all, even though you want to—you've got a sex hang-up.

In addition to frigidity and impotence there are, of course, numerous other types of sexual hang-ups. In this chapter, I will tell you about them.

Origins of Sexual Problems

The results of sexual molesting, rape, sexual caressing, and sexual teasing of a child will manifest themselves in later life in many different ways, but always as a sex hang-up.

If any of the above mentioned traumas happened before 3½ years of age, it will have become a part of programming, and the consequences will be considered *norm.* It will become a habit or a needed fantasy or even a needed pain, if pain was a part of the trauma.

If the same occurred after age 3½, it will have become an active memory of the child's consciousness and will manifest itself later in life as guilt or as fear. If sexual mistreatment starts before 3½ and also continues thereafter, the *"after* age 3½" attitude toward sex will prevail in later life. Guilt and fear will be felt even more strongly because the sexual desire, activated so early in life, will be felt that much more strongly.

	8 Categories Underlying Sex Problems		
	Situation	Age	Case
1.	father–daughter	under age 3½	Anna
2.	father–daughter	over age 3½	Lynn
3.	father–son	under age 3½	Amalio
4.	father–son	over age 3½	Randall
5.	mother–daughter	under age 3½	Joan
6.	mother–daughter	over age 3½	Lucille

| 7. | mother–son | under age 3½ | Aron |
| 8. | mother–son | over age 3½ | Robert/Abe |

The following situations and case histories are very "black and white" illustrations. Generally, there is, of course, a lot more gray.

---

1. Father–Daughter, under age 3½
If she is raped, sexually attacked, or mistreated by her father (or any other man) she will have the need for a violent type of intercourse in her later life. She will only, at best and without violence, reach a climax if she can fantasize that she is being raped.

Anna   Age 45, assistant to a pharmacist, married once for one year.

Her problem: Terrified of men. Her sexual experiences, although few, were accompanied by fantasies of rape. She hates sexual intercourse, and lives in constant fear of men who will rape her. Yet, she stands nude in front of her window, challenging the very thing she fears most.

Root of her problem: Her father was a cruel man in many ways. He took her frequently into a dim-lit room. He then approached her with his trousers down and exposed his penis. He put his hands on her little body and raped her. Sometimes Anna was forced by her father to lick the inside of his anus and suck his penis.

Family background: A well-established, well-educated, cultured, orthodox, God-fearing middle-class family. Her mother was deeply involved in social and church affairs. Her father was a bank executive.

---

2. Father–Daughter, over age 3½
If she has had sexual relations or was sexually fondled by her father (or any other man), the daughter will not be able to have normal sex relations in her later life. Fear and guilt will inhibit her potential sexual happiness.

Lynn   Age 35, librarian, twice divorced, one child who was given up for adoption.

Her problem: Unhappy with life, cannot relax while having sexual intercourse. Never had a climax. Aggressive in her attitude with men.

Root of her problem: We discovered that she was sexually molested by her father while standing between her father's legs while he was sitting on the couch in their living room. She had to give him oral satisfaction while he kept his hands on her buttocks, Even the memory of the odor of the discharge came back to her.

For this reason in her adult life she had to wash her mouth after each intercourse. She had often wondered about her own behavior because without the memory of the past, it had never made any sense.

When she was twelve and her breasts had started to develop, her mother took her to her father, where Lynn had to stand in front of him. Father was sitting on the chair and Lynn had to show her breasts. Then her father proceeded to caress them. Mother watched.

Family background: Father and mother were both teachers. He was also a principal.

---

3. Father–Son, under age 3½
If his penis was touched or played with by his father (or any other man), it will become part of the boy's programming. Therefore, in later life, another man playing with his penis will equal Norm and it will feel good. It may result in homosexual tendencies.

Amalio   Age 45, Department store buyer, twice divorced.

His problem: He takes the blame for everything. He thinks that he is the cause for everything that spells trouble. He is primarily homosexual, but frequently goes to bed with women.

Root of his problem: His father hated him but was proud of Amalio's penis. He told and showed the whole neighborhood how big his son's penis was. As a matter of fact, Amalio's crowded neighborhood was glued together with anything and everything having to do with sex. All the children and all the adults constantly had sex together. Amalio himself had his first sex when he was seven with his Aunt Rosalie, and from then on, every day. Mother said that sex was OK. His father said that it was wrong. His father, however, kept playing with his son's penis, of which he was so proud.

Family background: Hard-working people in a typical New York ethnic neighborhood.

> **4. Father–Son, over age 3½**
> If the father (or any other man) plays with or hurts his son's genitals, the boy will develop an urge to fight. But he won't because he fears his father (or the other man). As a result, in later life, he will automatically fear that every man with whom he is emotionally involved, will attack him.

Randall   Age 25, delivery man. Married with three children.

His problem: Fear of men. In his mind every man is a homosexual. He is fearful of relating to or even touching his own children.

Root of his problem: His father was always caressing Randall's penis. Sometimes his father and mother took sunbaths in the nude. Randall then sat on his father's lap. Father had a hard-on and they played together sexually. The feeling Randall got was nauseating, yet exciting.

Family background: "The Bible is the Word of God and the only Truth in our home." This typified Randall's family. He was brought up with constant fear of the Devil and of burning in Hell. "Your body is the Temple of God," was his mother's frequent quote.

> **5. Mother–Daughter, under age 3½**
> If the mother (or any other woman) mistreats her daughter sexually, the daughter may be sexually attracted to women in her later life. This will then result in lesbian tendencies.

Joan   Age 30, sales person in a travel agency, single.

Her problem: She was a lesbian, her motto: "Sex is better with girls, less trouble . . . same climax." One day, unsuspectingly, she fell in love with a man.

Root of her problem: Joan's mother never slept with her husband in the same bed. She slept with Joan since the time Joan was a baby. Mother fondled her sexually. She took her young daughter with her in the bathtub for sexual play.

Family background: Father a college professor, mother a housewife.

---

6. Mother–Daughter, over age 3½
When a mother (or any other woman) sexually mistreats her daughter, it may create a hatred for women, as well as compulsive jealousy, in her later life. It may manifest itself in nude or near-nude exposure in public, or in the wearing of extravagant clothing, showing much of her female attributes.

Lucille Age 24, Las Vegas showgirl, single.

Her problem: Fear of older women she doesn't know. Thinks that every woman will treat her as a whore. She fights women in authority and gets in trouble. (She does not have this problem with women her own age.)

Root of her problem: When Lucille was 5 her mother died. About a year later her father remarried. Lucille was an extremely beautiful little girl and therefore a sore in the eyes of her jealous stepmother. Lucille was regularly beaten by her and threatened that she would be killed if she told her father.

Family background: Stepmother housewife, father dentist.

---

7. Mother–Son, under age 3½
If the mother (or any other woman) plays sexual games with her son, he will, as an adult, always be specifically attracted to those parts of the female anatomy which were predominantly exposed and used by his mother in their sexual play. He will be attracted only by those women who duplicate his mother's physical appearance. The sequence of making love between mother and son will be compulsively repeated with his wife in his later life. If his mother took the initiative, then he will wait for his wife to do the same.

Aron Age 40, life insurance salesman, divorced with two children.

His problem: Uncontrolled laughter during intercourse and difficulty in breathing when sexually excited.

Pressure on his penis and testicles produces hysterical laughing, making breathing difficult. Even when Aron listens to a joke about "grabbing balls," he can't control his laughter.

Root of his problem: When Aron was a baby, his mother used to tickle his penis and testicles so that the baby would laugh. Then she could show off her "happy" son to her friends.

Through third party information, it became known that his mother still does similar things today. This time, however, she tickles the balls of her poodle.

Family background: Well-to-do. Father is a manufacturer of ladies' garments. Mother is a socially active housewife.

---

8. Mother–Son, over age 3½
If the mother (or any other woman) has a sexual relationship with or plays sexually with her son, it will result in impotence in later life, especially with the woman he really and truly loves. Not necessarily with a woman he doesn't care about or with a prostitute.

Robert Age 60, aeronautical engineer, married three times, no children.

His problem: He can have sex with any woman but after he gets emotionally involved, falls in love with her and marries her, he becomes impotent.

Root of his problem: Robert's mother was a big, strong woman. From the age of six, Robert slept in bed with his mother. She first took his penis in her mouth and then proceeded to put his penis in her vagina. They had intercourse regularly. When he was lying next to her, he always had to wait till she started. Sometimes she did, sometimes she didn't. When Robert is with a woman now, he will wait till *she* starts. It is impossible for him to take the initiative.

Family background: His father was a cowboy in Montana. His mother could drive a team of six horses.

8b. Mother–Son over age 3½

Abe Age 35, owns his own appliance repair shop, single.

His problem: Sexually inhibited, cannot reach a normal climax.

Root of his problem: While father and mother were in bed together, mother took Abe on top of her, put her nipple in his mouth, and let him suck her breast while slowly rubbing his body against hers. His father smiled. Abe's desire to have sexual intercourse with his mother was, at such moments, extremely strong but never fulfilled.

[While in therapy, reliving his trauma, he fantasized himself into actually having intercourse with his mother, something he had wanted to happen thirty years before.]

Family background: Very nice, warm, upper-middle class family. A family one would be proud to have as friends or neighbors.

Frigidity and Impotence

Let's talk about frigidity and impotence because that will lead to the exercises for other sexual problems as well. I will use the case history of Pat because it is such a typical one. There are, of course, countless variations on this theme. The reader must realize that in Patricia's case, although it happens to be one of a heterosexual male Helper together with a heterosexual female Subject, SpeyerMethod will work, of course, in case of females helping females or males helping males or females helping males. It is simply a matter of two *persons* working together.

PATRICIA

"Am I frigid?" Patricia asked with a pale face. "Yes, Pat, you are," I answered, "but when we talk about frigidity it's because of the lack of a better word. I consider a woman frigid (or a man impotent) if she cannot reach a sexual orgasm at the time she desires it while having sex under normal circumstances, stimulation and position. Let me give you a definition of what I consider 'normal' ideal circumstances."

1. *Circumstances:* A woman must have lived together (sharing territory) with the man she loves for at least six consecutive months. She must have intercourse at least several times a week. She must have a desire for sex of her own free will. There must not be any physical or mental illness. Both partners must be aware of each other and of the sex act in which they are involved.
2. *Stimulation:* The norm for stimulation is that foreplay must precede the actual intercourse in order to start the upward curve of excitement.
3. *Position:* The woman lies on her back, in a comfortable bed and the man is on top of her. They face each other. Both partners are nude. The man penetrates the woman's vagina with a completely erect penis. He should have his ejaculation in such a period of time as enables his partner to reach her climax. It is not necessary that both partners reach their climaxes at exactly the same moment.
4. *The partner:* It is a requisite, of course, that the partner be normal in his sexual behavior and potential.

Very important It must be very clearly understood that a climax may be reached under entirely different circumstances, stimulation, position and even without a partner (masturbation). But we are talking here about a woman who has tried everything to no avail. Therefore, if she is still frigid under the above-mentioned "ideal" circumstances, she has, most likely, a sexual hang-up and is frigid as a result of it.

Warning #13: "Pat," I continued, "you have to see your physician first and if there is nothing wrong with you medically, we'll start the SpeyerMethod."

Warning #14: The SpeyerMethod must be carried out with the true welfare of the partnership in mind. Both partners must accept the idea that sex is perfectly normal and healthy, a necessary function of the body, and that sex is not wrong, not dirty, not sacrilegious, and should not create feelings of guilt, sin, pain, or duty.

But since the subject *is* frigid (impotent), one or more of these negative feelings must rule her/his sex life.

Intellectually, however, she/he should not have any of these objections about sex.

Back to Pat and Her Sex Problem   Let's go back to Patricia. Pat had been happily married for the past three years but had never had a climax in her life. Let's get some information about Pat's life, including the circumstances which created her frigidity hang-up.

Pat is one of those wholesome young women who is followed by the eyes of every man who sees her. She is a TV starlet in Hollywood and lives in a world of glamour. Her early childhood, though, had not been glamorous at all. She grew up on a ranch just outside a small California town. Her father was an extremely strict person; her mother was hypocritical and jealous; her four brothers, wild. Mom always warned her against sex and from the time Pat was a little girl, Mom told her cruel and creepy stories about it. She said things like: "You are going to be stoned to death if you go to bed with a man before you are married."

As a child, Pat sensed the no-love situation at home. She was left alone quite a bit. How much left alone is told in the following details of her case history.

They are, at the same time, your instructions on how to proceed.

But *first*
heed the warnings #2 and #3
on page 29
then
follow the instructions, warnings and observations
on page 39 through 44
including
steps #1 through #23, page 43–44

Patricia was lying on my office bed, blindfolded and relaxed.

"Pat," I said, "I am going to touch you on various places on your body. We are going to find the obstacle, the blockage, the inhibition, and the fear that blocks the road of communication between your brain and your vagina. Anything sexually abnormal that ever might have happened to you when you were little lies registered in your skin and in your muscles and is filed in your brain."

However, before giving you, the helper, specific instructions on how to proceed with your subject, let's—again—realize that touching vagina and penis in order to alleviate sex traumas, may cause many to have "second thoughts" about it, helper as well as subject.

Therefore, let's first listen to another scenario: It is today, the Nineties. Suddenly news services flash the following event on national TV. "It has been discovered that a religious cult in the Middle East brutally cut—with a razor sharp knife—the skin on the head of the penis of every eight day old baby boy, born in that tribe.

"It is done by a lay person without any form of anesthesia. At the same time, parents, family and friends are looking on."

Can you imagine what kind of turmoil this news item would create, at this point in time.

So here is an important note to helper and subject alike:

1. The most important thing in this exercise is *the touch*. The subject, involved in his or her problem, with eyes closed, does *not* feel "a hand" but feels only pressure.
2. If it makes all parties more comfortable, use a small pillow instead of your hand.
3. Because it is the pressure that counts, it makes no difference if the helper is a male and the subject is a female. Or, by the

> same token, it could be a male helping a male or a female helping a female or male.

Instructions to Helper

1. You put your hand on the following places on your subject's body, one spot at a time, softly, without much pressure, announcing first that you are going to do it.
2. Helper: "I am going to put my hand on your right breast. Tell me the first thing that comes to your mind."

   Go on with touching the other breast, shoulders, arms, buttocks, hair, ears, cheeks, vagina (penis), thighs, etc.

   But besides touching, you have to test the other senses too.

   Say to your subject while doing the touching: "What do you *hear?*" "What do you *see?*" "What do you *smell?*" You will ask these questions only when you have some sort of negative reaction from your subject, while you have your hand on a certain spot on his/her body.

   When I touched the inside of Pat's right thigh, I said, as I had said before when touching her:
3. "Feel my hand and tell me the first thing that comes to your mind." Her first answer was: "Nothing."
4. I applied a little more pressure, as I had done in other places and said:
5. "Feel my hand and tell me what pictures come to your mind."

   Pat whispered: "I become frightened."
6. "What are you afraid of, Pat?" Pat: "I don't know."
7. "Feel that fright, Pat, and keep giving me your thoughts."

   Pat's voice was very low and hardly audible: "I am being held down."

   "Who is holding you down, Pat?" "I don't know" "Feel his hand, Pat, look at his arms, look at his shoulders, who is he?"

   "I don't know, but he has dark hair."
8. "You still feel my hand on your right thigh Pat. Now tell me where do you feel my other hand?" "It's not your hand. It's a body, laying on top of me. I'm so frightened."
9. Pat started to cry and shake.
10. I encouraged her to cry and shake and be aware of her feelings of fear.

11. After a while Pat was exhausted and felt totally drained. I let her relax, rest and breathe in deeply, three times (as in #21 and #22 on page 44)

    It was quite apparent now that something wrong had happened to her when she was a little girl.

12. I put my hand on her other thigh. She had no associations whatsoever. "It just feels sort of good," she said.

13. After you have reached this stage, the next step is to put your finger on your subject's vagina, press and rub slightly. Remember, your finger is on top of her clothes.

14. Ask her: "When you feel my finger, what's the first thing that comes to mind?"

15. Give her time if there is a negative answer, even if there is no answer. Pat said: "I feel pain."

16. If there *is* a reaction, say: "Keep feeling that pain and feel it as terribly as you can and tell me what comes to your mind."

    In Pat's case, a memory came back of a bladder infection that had caused pain and had not been attended to by her parents.

17. While rubbing on top of her vagina with one hand, put your other hand on several other places on her body, like lower belly, thighs, breasts, lips, places possibly touched when sexually assaulted. This, in order to try to get more reactions and trauma memories.

18. When I reached her lips and tried to put my finger on them, she clenched her teeth. She felt a blind fright and her whole body shook.

19. She pushed my hand away from her lips and I let her do that repeatedly. We now have a combination of three "reaction-touch-areas": 1. inside right thigh; 2. on the vagina; and 3. the lips. I put my finger again on her lips, kept it there and asked: "Tell me what you feel and see, Pat."

20. "I feel some man pulling my head between his legs. He is tall, has dark hair, and a long nose."

21. When we reached this moment, Pat was totally exhausted from fear, fighting, disgust and revulsion.

22. She cried, raved, tried to break away and actually *re-lived* in her mind, at that very moment, something terrible that had happened to her in her early childhood.

    Let her fight! Use the pillow.

    Pat remembered the whole scene. A babysitter had sexually molested her. "I remember lying on my back, with him on top of me. He was masturbating between my legs. I could hardly breathe because of his weight. And it smelled terrible. While I was lying in that awful position, I constantly looked at our piano in the living room. This explains," Pat interrupted herself, "why I have this life-long dislike of pianos!"

Some More Instructions

23. While your subject is reliving some nasty experiences, and that may be moments *before* she/he starts talking about it, don't give your subject comfort at all, don't soothe her/him. Nor should you let her/him get up and move away from the bed. Use your pillow to let her/him fight. To her the pillow is the rapist.
24. She must stay on the bed. (From now on she also means he.)
25. When she is in agony she may fight, kick, shout or rave.
26. Don't hold her down but let her fight against the pillow. It all has to come out.
27. Whatever happens, *keep talking to her!* Keep in communication with her. Do that by encouraging her to shout and fight. *She must hear your voice at all times!*
28. These kinds of outbursts will be ended by her or, if they last more than 30 to 40 minutes, by you.
29. The exercises have to be repeated, at least until your subject feels sort of "empty." This may take 30 to 40 minutes each day and may last several days (the average is between 2 and 5 days).
30. If, at moments, you cannot hold her during her raving and her fighting, you say: *"relax . . . relax"* and *take off her eyemask.* Tell her to *open her eyes* and look around in the room. Let her tell you *what* she sees, like a plant, a painting, a chair. These are your safety valves.
31. *Again:* Put your hand over her vagina and if her reaction is once more one of irritation, anger or fear, let her push away those negative feelings by pushing away your hand (or the pillow) from the vagina, pubic, and thigh areas.
32. After the fear is more or less gone, there will appear a feeling of anger. Let her get angry at the rapist, or even at her parents if that comes spontaneously.
    Tell her to use all her *willpower* to beat away her negative feelings but *be specific.* She must name *who or what* she is fighting.
33. Tell her to continue to beat and/or scream until *she* feels that everything has evaporated from her memory . . . *but!*

34. Moments later, let her do it all over again until *you* are satisfied, that whatever you do, no more reaction will surface.
35. You will have to come to a point where your subject likes the feel of your hand on her vagina/his penis.
36. While the helper was not allowed to give his subject any form of sympathy during the actual reaction periods, after the session is over, give her/him all the sympathy and human love you have. Embrace her/him.

We go back once again to Pat and listen some more to what she has to say: "I was afraid to tell all this to my mother because the babysitter threatened to kill me if I did."

Pat's mother was a hypocritical woman, anti-sex-minded, and has told her daughter from her early childhood on, in no uncertain terms, the atrocities Pat would experience if she did not adhere to "Golden Rules" of sexual behavior. Without any doubt, all this contributed to the fact that Pat never told anyone about being molested.

Had she had a different type of mother, one who might have taught her children that sex was pleasant and perfectly normal, Pat would have told her parents and the culprit might have been caught . . . the culprit, who might have come back to do it again, or perhaps, went on to some other innocent child.

In other cases, where the mother is understanding, the child may still be afraid to tell because of an unreasonably strict or jealous father. Patricia, at this stage of her life and having experienced the SpeyerMethod, is perfectly capable of getting an orgasm. She feels she is a real woman now. She told me how beautiful it feels to be aware of that fact.

Exercises

Not all cases are as dramatic as Pat's, although some are much worse. Milder cases, such as those in which the father and the mother only have an anti-sex attitude or sing the "Sex = Sin" song, can still cause the same degree of frigidity, however. When during the SpeyerMethod all traumas and traumatic memories are re-lived and released, your subject will undergo a definite change of attitude, even of personality. Many other obstacles and inhibitions have been the result of the sex trauma. The parental attitude also influenced your subject's total behavior not only her/his sexual relations.

Once the original trauma is re-lived and the parental attitude is abreacted (discharged) some more exercises are still necessary to help your subject fully enjoy his/her new-found sexuality.

Touch

- Again, helper and subject assume the same position as before.
- Make sure that your subject is relaxed.
- Rub your subject's vagina (penis) until she/he becomes sexually excited.
- If she/he can't get sexually excited, just let her/him feel the warmth of your hand through her/his clothes.
- If that is still difficult, keep your full hand on her vagina (his penis) until she (he) feels the warmth, even if it is only a fraction of a second. (We will continue to use "she," but it is, of course, "he" when applicable.)
- Now say to your subject in a low, soft voice: "Feel my finger (or hand), feel excited, let yourself go. Just concentrate on that beautiful feeling." But please, helper, use your own words, not mine.
- While continuing the rubbing of her vagina and she is concentrating on her feeling of sexual excitement, or warmth,
- suddenly say, with a hard, loud voice: "Stop that feeling, fight that good feeling, freeze it, don't feel anything!"
- But keep rubbing her vagina (his penis) while you say these words.
- Now go back to your soft voice again—keep rubbing—and tell the subject to get excited again.
- Keep alternating between *feel it* and *freeze it* or *feel it* and *fight it*, softly rubbing all the time.
- Your subject must become aware of her alternating feelings of her true sexual excitement and, on the other hand, of her fear of it.
- You must make sure that during the course of these sessions the subject gets fully involved in her feeling of sexual excitement and just as fully involved in her feeling of frigidity. After going through these exercises, talk together about the subject's reactions. Whatever happens, once you have started this SpeyerMethod, you *must* finish it, regardless of how many sessions it may take.

Very important It is *not* necessary that your subject gets the exact memory back of circumstances involving specific persons or specific actions surrounding the cause of the trauma. As long as he/she reacts to the exercise and the exercise appears to be successful—meaning that the helper's touch has eventually become meaningless—the subject could have either remembered the trauma in detail, part of it, have fantasized about it, or have no memory of it at all.

When she/he reacts to the touch, the problem areas will be cleared of fear and pain and consequently her/his problem will disappear.

Trouble Touch

Some people have certain areas on the body which, when touched, even lightly, cause fear, pain, or irritation. This will happen anytime when involved in the sex act. It could occur before, after, or during coitus.

For some people this fear or this pain is so strong that when the helper as much as suggests that he is going to touch that problem spot, but in reality is not touching it, the fear, pain, or irritation is already felt.

The typical problem areas are: Breasts, nipples (sometimes a very precise location on the breast or nipple), lips, lower abdomen, the pubic hair area, the area surrounding the vagina, the vagina itself, the inside of one or both thighs, the penis, the scrotum, the testicles, the buttocks and the anus. Sometimes certain words or circumstances may cause fear, pain or irritation. Even certain smells or tastes may produce asexual feelings.

All these trouble-touch areas have a history. Someone or something started it.

By putting your hand or your finger on the exact spot, the subject will relive the fear, pain, or irritation—if not immediately, then in time.

The Switch System

A female subject has the following sexual problem: Any time a penis touches the outside of her vagina or her vaginal lips, her vaginal muscles go into a spasm and the penis cannot enter the vagina.

Exercise: The helper puts his/her finger on the subject's vagina, exerting a little pressure so that the subject will be aware of "something" about to enter her vagina. Since your subject is fully clothed, the pressure of your finger just means pressure to her and does *not* specifically mean your finger.

Next you say to your blindfolded subject: "Feel the touch of a penis on your vagina. Become aware, when you feel this penis, how you contract and tighten your muscles." Be sure that she *is* aware of what she is doing. Move your finger off the vagina for a second, then move it back and say: "Now you feel *my finger* on your vagina . . . relax your muscles." Make sure, by asking her, that her muscles are relaxed. Next you repeat the exercise, switching between "feel a penis—contract" and "feel my finger—relax."

Rhythmic Counting

Helper puts his finger (hand) on the vagina and says: "Feel my finger—relax . . . two . . . three . . . four." Remove your finger for a moment, put it back and say: "Feel a penis—contract (your muscles) . . . two . . . three . . . four." Keep doing this until you feel that the contraction of the vaginal muscles is becoming more difficult to do on your rhythmic commands. Eventually it will be impossible for her to contract them. Your subject will indicate the progress by telling you how she experiences her feeling about the muscle contractions. Thereafter, you may also do this exercise *without* the blindfold. You show her your finger, let her touch your finger on its way to the vagina. When you tell her that your finger is a penis she will contract her vaginal muscles. When you tell her: "Now, it's my finger," she will not mind the touch on her vagina.

Anything goes, as long as the blocked subconscious trauma can be made conscious. And that's exactly what we are doing!

A female subject has the following sexual problem: During sex the vagina stays dry or part of the vagina begins to hurt, all because of traumatic fears. (Remember, the subject already checked with her doctor to make sure that there is no current medical problem.)

The origins of such traumas may be a guilt feeling imposed by the parents, or the Sex = Sin theme taught by some religions, sexual fondling or caressing by one or both parents, punishment involving the genitals, painful sexual play with other children, rape, incest, accidents, medical treatment, operations, or sadistic treatment by parents or other persons.

"Healthy" Incest

Sometimes a little girl and her father or a little boy and his mother have an unspoken, unmanifested "love affair" which is almost always sensed by the parent and child alike, although on a subconscious level. The contact between the two "lovers" is always through the *eyes*. The parent may be either warm, touchy and affectionate, or cold, distant and unaffectionate. While the parent usually is completely unaware of the sexual connotation of this "eye" relationship with his or her child, the little boy or girl *will* register it as a request and a desire for sex by the parent of the opposite sex (same sex with homosexuals). The child would like to respond, of course, but doesn't.

In later life, this subconscious incestuous desire may cause emotional and/or sexual problems. Your subject will always go after—and fall in love with—the typical father or mother figure.

Incest Exercise   Your subject is blindfolded and lies on her back. We'll do this exercise for a female subject. For a male, it's nearly identical, with only a difference in father/mother words and, later on, the position on the bed and the climax.

Ask your subject to look into her father's eyes (the male subject looks into his mother's eyes). Ask her what she feels. She may want to push away her father's eyes. Let her! Use the pillow.

Now suggest the following to her: "Feel your father's eyes on your hair, his eyes are moving to your forehead. Feel his eyes on your eyes, on your lips. His eyes are inspecting your breasts (skip this part for male subjects), going down to your vagina (penis), your thighs."

This time, don't ask for reactions. She has to get involved in the sensual and sexual feelings associated with her father's (his mother's) eyes. Ask the subject questions such as where it felt best and where it was the most exciting.

Either one of two things can happen: 1. The subject will react violently against her father, 2. She will react with a desire to make love to him. Reaction 1 is usually followed by 2.

In both cases, let the subject fully react. For case 1, let her get rid of her fears. For case 2, put the pillow on top of her chest and tell her to put her arms around her father (the pillow). Let her talk to him, expressing her love. Then put another pillow, between her legs and let her make love to her father. In the beginning, you may have to coax your subject to do this. Then just wait until she indicates that it is all over. Some subjects may actually climax, but most of them digest the climax in the brain, although strong sexual feelings, and some sexual body movements are sometimes observable by the helper.

If your subject wants to remove the pillow, let her. Let her do the entire exercise *her way.* Once she is on the way to fulfilling that childhood desire, let her finally do it however she feels like.

But whatever happens, never take off her mask!

The same goes for a male subject. At the last stage, however, you put him gently onto his belly, pillow between his legs. He'll take it from there. Do this exercise with your subject several times, over a number of days. Some feel they don't need to repeat this exercise anymore after the first time; others want to go on forever.

As a helper, you have to tell those who want to go on "forever" to do so by themselves, at home. You gave them the choreography, now let them do the dancing.

In cases of married people or lovers you must tell your woman subject to ask her husband or boy friend to cooperate by playing the role of "her Daddy" while making love together. She must also call him "Daddy" during these intimate moments. The same, of course, goes for your male subject, whose wife or girl friend will play the role of his "Mommy." Fulfillment of the subconscious childhood sex wish is, at the same time, the end of the trauma.

Some do not consider this a trauma. I know of several cases where father and daughter or mother and son have continued their relationships far into adult life. But who is to sit in judgment?

Re-Living a Rape

This involves the same exercises as for the other sexual problems, although in a rape case, the emphasis should be on the physical fight against the rapist. Here, age is of no consequence. This exercise is for victims of rape, at whatever age it may have occurred.

To begin, the helper must activate the memory of the rape. He puts his finger on the lower abdomen of the female subject. Then, you, the helper start your journey with your touching finger, going slowly in the direction of her vagina. Let *her* indicate the exact route your finger should take. The subject must guide your finger: "A little more to the right, a little lower," etc. Put your other hand on her breast. Again, let her indicate where the rapist touched or hurt her. In this way, you will eventually find the exact spots on her body and the position of her body during the rape scene. It will then become possible for your subject to re-live the rape and get rid of her fears and the sexual and emotional problems that are still connected with it.

The fight against your hands, arms and pillow will be of tremendous power, regardless of the age, weight or size of the rape victim. All the insult, anger, and need for revenge, as well as the feeling of having one's own most intimate territory violated, will eventually come out with all the force the rape victim possesses.

Zex (Zero Sex) Exercises for Impotent Males

First do the touch exercises, the same as for women, including "feel it or freeze it."

- He lies on the bed, on his back, blindfolded.
  Tell him the following fantasy story:
- "In your fantasy, you see that I (the helper) have a sharp knife in my hand (pause) . . .
- when I count to three . . . I am going to cut off your penis . . . (pause and take the pillow in your hand)
- *one . . . two . . . three."*

- On the count of *three,* drop and push with some force the pillow onto the subject's penis.
- Your subject will jump up, scream, and fight off the "knife."
- Let him defend himself against castration, let him fight (the pillow).
- Encourage him to fight and scream.
- Repeat until he finds the whole thing has become senseless and he doesn't react any longer when he hears your story or when you drop the pillow between his legs.

The same castration exercise may also be used with a female subject who wants to castrate her father, brother, or any other man. Let her do it in her fantasy-play. In this case, however, she has to re-enact the castration ritual. So, give her a stick or anything else that feels like a knife in her hand. The same exercise can be used for homosexuals who want to castrate their fathers, ex-lovers, or friends.

All Purpose Exercise

Put your hand on your subject's genital area, or push your finger against his anus (for homosexuals).

Let him or her feel fear, pain, or irritation.

Tell him or her to push away the pain and let him keep pushing and fighting your hand (or pillow) until the pain, fear, or irritation have disappeared.

Repeat the same exercises again the next day to be sure that the hang-up has disappeared. The helper may combine this exercise with letting the subject say out loud the name of the culprit involved: His father, mother, a priest, God, the doctor, a brother, a sister, a relative, a neighbor, or a stranger. Sometimes the culprit is even an animal, an object, a thing, or a dramatic happening.

At Last . . . the Climax

After the SpeyerMethod has been applied, the subject's actual climaxing may start soon thereafter, certainly within the next month. In some exceptional cases it may take six months, however. All this is determined—in a very strong measure—by the sincere feelings that the subject has for the partner.

When a woman who was frigid, or a man who was impotent, is now able to climax, she and he will still be easily distracted from the sex act. A no-climax intercourse may still occur when circumstances are not all "perfect."

If the climaxing has not started by the second month after the SpeyerMethod has been completed, the subject should stop having sex for about a week and then the helper should start some of the exercises once more.

"Mood and Circumstances" can be powerful distractions to the sex act, and not only for the formerly frigid!

But, whatever, *don't give up till it works,* regardless of how many times you have to do it all over again.

As a result of the SpeyerMethod, your subject will go through some personality changes in addition to the newly achieved sexual freedom and independence. Now that many obstacles and inhibitions have been removed, a freer person emerges.

The Reaction ... Short and Long Term

The subject may at first get very angry at her father or whoever the culprit of her sexual agony might have been.

It is very important to realize that changes have taken place in your subject's body *and* mind. There are bound to be reactions. These reactions may manifest themselves as a depressed feeling, as some sort of protest, or as a feeling of rejection.

In most cases this reaction is directed towards the subject's partner and/or the father or mother. It will also show up in relationships with their children, friends, neighbors, and even at work.

As a matter of fact, this reaction *has* to come! and when it does, the helper may congratulate him- or herself. It's the indicator of a success. A low point, however, may be expected in the middle of the second month after SpeyerMethod was finished. Such a low point may include being frigid (impotent) again. But when it happens at that particular time, it will go back to normal again in about two days.

> Re-read pages 49 through 52
> the 3-months after-wave reaction
> Hosanna *and* Hallelujah . . .
> . . . but not yet

It is important to note that the initial excitement of being a helper and whatever sexual feelings it may have activated in the beginning will, by this time, have disappeared. Rubbing a vagina or a penis becomes as ordinary as waxing your car, or ironing a garment.

Libido

Libido—kinetic sexual energy—plays an important role; the intensity of the hang-up depends on it.

"Libido" is the inherited amount of electricity (energy) we all have in our brain and body. It could also be translated as "expressiveness." It manifests itself not only sexually but emotionally and intellectually as well. Children with a high libido (lots of energy, but not quite hyper) are more easily given problems by defective parents than children with a low libido. The inhibitions parents saddle them with are much more difficult to hold inside because the high libido child has a much greater need to express himself.

Low libido children can take the parental abuse more easily. Their pressure to express themselves is somewhat lower.

As a result, high libido adults are bothered by their sexual hang-ups more so than low libido adults are.

The tragedy is that one can't *see* a libido when it is inhibited. Our sex drive manifests itself in various degrees of intensity. A person can be (1) normal, (2) under-sexed or (3) over-sexed. This degree of intensity is usually inherited.

When parents inhibit their children's sex drive, whether it be by fear, guilt or molesting, the chance of being frigid, impotent in later life is considerable.

When a highly sexed or over-sexed person has been inhibited by his parents, and if the inhibitions are reinforced in his married or adult life—which is usually the case—he may end up developing cancer. Furthermore, breast cancer is believed to occur with greater frequency in sexually frustrated women. (This frustration must have been ongoing for ten to twenty years or so, not just a weekend.) The electricity (energy) created by sexual excitement, which would normally exit the body through the system of orgasm, is now forced to seek its exit through other means such as haphazard cell division.

The fact that breast cancer may occur in sexually frustrated women does *not!!* automatically indicate that all frustrated women will develop cancer. But who wants to take the chance . . .

Hi – Lo – Libido

Marriage partners or lovers may each be born with a different intensity of sex drive, also known as libido. The following situations may then occur:

Man	Woman	
Hi	Hi	No problem
Lo	Lo	No problem
Hi	Lo	Little problem. He wants sex more frequently than she. She may protest but, if "necessary," she can accept it. She can be passive while he is active.
Lo	Hi	Big problem. She wants sex more frequently than he. He must be more active to satisfy her. He can't! She doesn't understand, insists on it. He loses his masculine self-image, inside and outside the bedroom. Big problem. Solution: Talk it out together, accept it as genetic and physical, *not* as emotional. He should give a little more (use his finger), she should ask a little less (occasionally masturbate), and both should be happy with IT and with each other.

Orgasms in Secrecy and in Fantasy

Bear in mind that the actual moments of an orgasm, although certainly very exciting, are as such not all that important. Yet, being able to reach an orgasm also represents being a real woman or a real man all the other hours of the day and night. Regardless of how feminine a frigid woman or how masculine an impotent man might be, they will be even more secure in their womanhood and masculinity when they are able to comfortably reach an orgasm.

In addition, sexual inhibitions are always coupled to emotional inhibitions. This, however, is not necessarily true the other way 'round.

Neither man nor woman should have an uncontrolled need for fantasies such as: Being raped, sex with another person in addition to or instead of the partner one is with at the moment, sex with animals, the need for pain or unusual positions, places or objects.

Sometimes a person has these thoughts and feels these needs and the partner doesn't know anything about it. These fantasies are sometimes a person's innermost secrets and he or she would be ashamed to share these fantasies with his or her partner or anyone else.

On the other hand, some women fake an orgasm or are just as happy without one, as long as their partner reaches his. It must be noted here that some women who are not capable of getting complete sexual gratification through orgasm will never tell their partner. And the husband (partner) often, because of his ignorance or sheer egoism, will never know that his wife is "frigid."

Any woman or man has the inherited need and right to be her/himself, and to give as she or he pleases. The purpose of the Speyer-Method is, therefore, to achieve as complete a happiness as is humanly possible. When you, as the helper, hear these fantasies for the first time in the process of doing the SpeyerMethod, you may not know how to react to them. To carry out your "helpership" successfully, you have to be prepared to learn things about sex and, also, about human life that you never knew existed. Learning about it on a commonsense level is good experience for future communication with your own partner and for your general outlook on life.

The Eyes and Ears Have It

In topless bars and in Las Vegas and Paris shows, the main course is always the bare-breasted show girl, prancing about on the stage. These shows are highlighted by the promising disrobing of an exotic stripper. *Nudity is what sells.*

Although these shows are equally frequented by men and women, it's the *male* customer who makes the show continue. The women who go are mostly those who accompany their date or husband. Others just go out of curiosity to find out "what the nude girl's got that they haven't got."

The male primarily goes to see the wealth of nude female bodies, displayed a few feet in front of him. While he sits there and watches the show, he makes up his mind which girl is going to be his favorite. He examines her breasts, her legs and whatever else he can grab with his *eyes.* He deliberates with himself whether he is going to take one of them to bed, or all of them; all at once, or one at a time, depending on his Libido (temperament).

With a woman it's a different story. She usually gets sexually excited through her *ears,* the emphasis lies on *hearing.*

Let's take a look at the audience at a Rock Concert or at any other "scream-type" music happening. Music makes women swoon, scream, and come unglued. They want to throw themselves at the lead singer and crave to be sexually possessed by him. And these women are not just teenagers. Other singers, from Caruso via Sinatra to Springsteen, have made women fall in love with them just by the sound of their voice.

Basic Observations

> Sexual excitement in the male is emphasized through his *eyes*, in the female through her *ears*.

A man gets sexually excited because of what he *sees*. A semi-nude or totally nude woman excites him. She creates a strong sexual desire. Sex symbols, regardless of their subtlety or vulgarity, always excite a male observer more than a female observer. Any man who says that he does not get excited has a hang-up or is a hypocrite, a homosexual or is senile. All female nudeness and near-nudeness entering a man's brain through his eyes gives an instant sexual reaction.

The emphasis lies in the *seeing*.

With a woman it's different. With her the emphasis lies on *hearing*. I stress here the word "emphasis" because to a lesser degree, it works naturally the other way 'round too.

What can we do with this knowledge in our day-to-day-bedroom life? A wife, knowing that her husband's eye is very vulnerable to the sight of her nude body, can create excitement by wearing perhaps a garter belt and a veil-like negligee, giving him the impression of the promise that lies beneath her garment. She can playfully tease and direct her husband's eye slowly to her naked flesh. He has gotten it so often so easily, why not make it a little more intriguing and mysterious this time? How about once every two weeks?

Not every man is so fortunate as to have the voice quality of a Presley. Yet, he can still create a sexually charged atmosphere through his voice. He can talk to her about romantic things, about the beauty of her body. She will be sexually excited when he whispers sweet things in her ear. The things he can whisper may be complete fantasy, it is his *sound* that turns the woman on. Of course, no stock market reports.

A couple knowing the use of these stimuli will have so much more gratification during the touch, foreplay and actual intercourse. They are bound to have a more intimate, closer relationship than ever before.

Ladies and Gentlemen Fornicate to Propagate

The fornicate-to-propagate process is acted out on the world's stage in many different ways, plays and games. Each culture has its own ceremonial procedures.

One man may approach his love object—at first—with a tremble in his voice. He may write poetry or bring her roses. Another man may be so afraid of the woman he desires that he won't even approach her. He consummates his love for her only in his fantasy. On the other side of the spectrum are men who are bold, rough, and sometimes downright uncouth in their approach to women. Some men's desire for women may be so bestial that they have only one thought on their mind: To rape the object of their lust.

Underneath men's roses-to-rape approach to women lies a fascinating biological story line. In this frame, what *is* female beauty? Beauty—always in the eye of the beholder—is a translation of a healthy womb. And, of course, having observed this through his eyes, he must then immediately proceed to deposit his sperm into that healthy womb, his biological contribution to the proper propagation of the human species.

But this is just the male aspect of the story. Now comes the female part. She says then, in her own biological language: "OK, buddy, if you want to deposit your sperm in my womb, I'll first have to check out the quality of your genes." And she has many ways of doing just that. For instance: "I never do it on the first date." With this she checks if he has enough determination to come back. Or: "I want to get to know you better before I go to bed with you." It is also possible that she doesn't like his physique or his body odor or his age. What she is looking for in the way of gene quality is: Physical and emotional health, and intellectual, financial, and territorial protection. In other words, the best possible qualities for survival. All this to protect the quality and the safety of her offspring, survival of the fittest!

This is why a man "grabs" with his *eyes* a woman by the womb. But he cannot proceed to deposit his sperm until the woman checks, with her *ears,* that man's genes.

The gentleman usually goes for health (body). The lady goes for quality (brain). With ladies, sex starts "between her ears," with gentlemen, "between his legs."

All this happens—indeed on a primitive biological level—before the fornication-to-propagation process is allowed to take effect.

Can you still go out on a date knowing all this nudeness-to-the-bone information? Of course, you can. Discuss it with your date and play-act it together and I assure you that you'll have the best and most interesting date of your life.

An authentic present from Mary to Dr. Speyer.

> Mary had a little hang-up,
> That would not let her climax.
> And not one man that Mary tried,
> Could make the poor girl relax.

> It followed her from bed to bed,
> Much to her dismay.
> But when she met a Doctor Speyer,
> He had so much to say.

> The Doctor put her on the couch,
> And analyzed her psyche.
> He made her talk and yell and cry,
> Until he found the right key.

> The cure it took a short 10 days,
> Much to her delight.
> Now Mary cannot get enough,
> And makes love throughout the night.

Chapter Five

BORN FREE?? . . . REALLY

Birth Trauma: A Mark for Life

Hardly any medical doctors, including the psychiatrist as well as the clinical psychologist and most other so-called counselors, have the knowledge to link a birth trauma to its particular symptom in later life. In most cases these symptoms are treated as "psychological disorders." (I do not include in birth traumas problems due to the use of alcohol and drugs during pregnancy or any other pregnancy anomaly.)

The process of giving birth does not always seem to run in a synchronous way between the mother and her about-to-be-born baby. All, or any type of asynchronization, known or unknown to the mother and her doctor, will cause—to say the least—unusual habits or attitudes in later life.

A dramatic example, of course, is the seven-month premature birth. But besides being born too early, one can be born too late, or upside down, or in a near-suffocating position. Long labor, as well as Caesarean birth, even pre-natal stress, or an overdose of anesthetics, will certainly influence behavior in later life. Whatever the case may be, all birth irregularities will cause some sort of problem later.

But, we have to go a step further. Even births-on-time may cause traumas in later life, because it seems that too often mother and baby do not agree on the appointed time of birth.

Sometimes the baby's brain sends instructions to its muscles to start the process of being born when the mother is not quite ready. Or vice versa, mother's muscles start to work but her baby isn't quite ready yet. One of the two participants is not cooperating at the point where cooperation is essential.

Some other traumas are caused immediately after birth. For instance: The mother does not supply milk (breast or bottle) according to the wishes of her baby. It could be that the mother gives too much milk or not enough; too frequently or not frequently enough; she may be nervous or impatient when feeding; or her milk may be sour. All that can cause problems for this baby in his later life.

Manifestations in Adult Life

Manifestations of birth traumas in adult life are numerous:

1. Physical/Mental

- one eats too much, sometimes to the point of obesity;
- one drinks too much, sometimes to a state of alcoholism;
- smokes too much;
- has a compulsion to take naps;
- cannot get up in the morning;
- sleeps when confronted with problems;
- is often tired without a good reason;
- gives up easily;
- gives up temporarily and starts all over again at some later point;
- doesn't start anything that requires an effort;
- slow in body movement;
- slowness in decision making;
- slowness in relating word to action;
- overactive;
- plays "the waiting game"—waits to take action;
- wants to take action, but doesn't.
- Pre-natal stress of the mother will cause constant stress in her child, when he reaches the age of 16. The now adult "child" will be looking for stress situations, regardless of reality or he creates stressful situations, regardless of need. He is constantly under stress without apparent reason.
- Cold hands and/or cold feet, elevated or high blood pressure, asthma, vertigo or even rheumatism could be the result of a birth trauma.
- A breathing problem or sleeping too much can be the result of premature birth.
- The result in later life of the so-called breech birth may manifest itself in the form of nightmares and fear of water.
- Long labor pains, over several days, when the baby has to w-a-i-t to be born, may produce slowness in relating thought to word and word to action.

2. In the Workplace/Hobby
Some about-to-be-born babies try to get out of their mother's womb on their own when they think that their time has come. But if the

mother's body doesn't let them out, they stage a fight to get out on their own. They will use their arms, legs, shoulders, one or all. In later life, these too-late-born adults have the need to use those specific muscles that were previously used in the womb. They may choose a profession or a hobby, not knowing that their "choice" was based on their birth trauma. The chosen work puts emphasis on "muscle-work." He or she may become a physical therapist or masseur. The "chosen" hobbies may be bicycling, skiing, or swimming.

If, in the womb, the brain's instruction to be born were sent to his fingers, he may have become a neurosurgeon or a violinist.

Others have "chosen" their work or hobby due to inappropriate feeding after birth. One may become a short-order cook or a nutritionist.

An overdose of anesthesia during the birth process may cause one to become a nurse or choose medical science as one's profession.

Sound and Music in the Womb

Any disturbance of the euphoric status-quo of the fetus will show up by age 16 as compulsive, stress-related behavior. Music, be it classical or pop, transmitted via the abdomen directly to the fetus, as some music-loving parents do, will create a compulsive or stress attitude toward music or rhythm in later life. On one hand, the now adult person is irritated with music (the kind that was programmed into him or her while a fetus). On the other hand, he or she "needs" music or rhythm in order to fall asleep or relax.

The only sounds a fetus is supposed to hear are the (scrambled) tones of his mother's voice. This sound will eventually become his "mother tongue." Any disturbance during his womb-time may create—among others—speech problems, autism, heart(beat) irregularity or compulsive yawning.

The Key Lies in the Dream

Dreams are often the key as to whether a birth trauma has had its influence. "Being in a place and can't get out" or "missing or near-missing appointments or departures" is usually such an indication.

Both born-too-soon as well as born-too-late adults often have identical attitudes toward "doing things." They both w-a-i-t and w-a-i-t.

The born-too-soon person doesn't want to take action as yet, and therefore doesn't.

The born-too-late person wants to take action but doesn't because somehow he is incapable of acting. So he too, w-a-i-t-s.

To a lay person and to most professionals these two attitudes *seem* the same.

In both cases, similar dreams recur over a long period of time sometimes for years. The born-too-soon's dream: He is in a room or any other kind of enclosed area. He does not want to get out. But, somehow, he is forced or pushed out. This produces a feeling of irritation and/or frustration. The born-too-late's dream: He or she is in a room or any kind of enclosure or even involved in a situation where he wants to get out of or wants to escape from, but cannot. He is held back by obstacles or people or time schedules or anything else that feels like a pressure, a fear, or a frustration.

In a dream the typical symbol for the birth process is "The Tunnel." He sees the tunnel or the sewer or something circular and elongated, either dry or wet, with a rough or smooth surface, light or dim.

There is always a "Light at the end of the Tunnel." He will be in the process of trying to reach that light. Sometimes he succeeds, sometimes he doesn't. Sometimes there are little obstacles, sometimes it's impossible. The dream may be accompanied by fear feelings.

A round body of water (e.g., a lake, sometimes a dry lake) symbolizes the womb. In real life he may be either fearful of or attracted to: tunnels, bridges, flying, or trains.

Warning #15: Having any of these symptoms or any that will be mentioned on the following pages does not necessarily mean that there was a birth trauma! On the other hand, if there was a birth trauma, one or more of these symptoms will show up.

Wouldn't it be interesting to check it out? Why not ask your mother how the birth process did develop. Unfortunately, many mothers don't recall or, if something unusual happened, don't want to talk about it. Others in the family often remember better.

To undo the birth trauma's influence, one should follow the instructions and exercises outlined on the following pages. But first, here is a list of unusual births and what they may do to you.

Unusual Births

---

1. *Too soon*   (not necessarily premature)
2. *Too late*   (with or without stress on the fetus' muscles)
3. *Breech*   (upside down)
4. *Navel string*   (around the neck)
5. *Dry*   (no fluid)
6. *Long labor*   (over several days)
7. *Anesthesia*   (usually an overdose, but not necessarily so)
8. *Fetal distress*   (e.g., near drowning in fluid or blood)
9. *Caesarean section*
10. *Sound*   (via abdomen into womb or after birth, while asleep)
11. *Pre-natal stress*   (of the mother)
12. *Cold delivery*   (room temperature)
13. *Wrong feeding*   (after birth—breast or bottle)
14. *One live twin*   (other twin died in womb or was not known to have existed)
15. *First time eyes are opened*   (at birth)
16. *Forced birth*   (hands or forceps)

Warning #16. The influence of a birth trauma always starts to show up around AGE 16 (give or take 6 months)!

---

1. Too soon   (Does not necessarily mean only prematurely)
   Manifestations in Later Life
   Mental/Physical
   • sleeps a lot
   • sleeps late in the a.m.
   • sleeps early in the p.m.
   • easily tired for no reason
   • difficulty getting out of bed
   • doesn't like bright lights
   • supersensitive hearing
   • death or suicide wish
   In the Workplace/Hobby
   • goes to bed (or bed-like surroundings) when confronted with problems
   • goes to bed (or bed-like surroundings) when under stress

- no or little initiative
- needs to be pushed
- doesn't start anything himself that requires efforts
- "I'll do it later" attitude (and he will do it)
- procrastinates

2. Too late   (A) fetus uses muscles in birth process
Manifestations in Later Life
   Mental/Physical
- specific muscles are always tense (usually arms, legs, shoulders, or fingers)
- need to exercise these specific muscles
- starts things but stops
- starts, stops, and starts all over again (same project) will succeed eventually
- high blood pressure
- elevated blood pressure and/or stress when awakening
- asthma
- rheumatism

   In the Workplace/Hobby
- starts things but gives up
- starts and re-starts same project
- will look for work/hobby emphasizing those specific muscles used in the womb: massaging – bicycling – skiing – swimming – molding – weight-lifting – physical therapy – play (finger) instruments

(B) Fetus does *not* use muscles in birth process
Manifestations in Later Life
   Mental/Physical
- slowness of body movements
- slow in relating thought to words and words to action
- stress

   In the Workplace/Hobby
- needs a waiting period before starting (e.g., a project)
- slow in decision making
- "let someone else do it" attitude

3. Breech   (upside down)
Manifestations in Later Life
   Mental/Physical
- nightmares

- fear of water
- fear of drowning
- fear of water on face (shower or swimming)
- breathing problems

In the Workplace/Hobby

- compulsive about water in work and hobby

4. Naval string   (around baby's neck)

Manifestations in Later Life

Mental/Physical

- breathing problems
- fear of choking
- fear of swallowing
- fear of suffocating
- can't stand to be touched on neck and throat

In the Workplace/Hobby

- wears high collars around neck (shirt – dress – shawl – sweater)
- compulsion to wear something around neck (scarf – jewelry) neck must always be covered

5. Dry   (no fluid)

Manifestations in Later Life

Mental/Physical

- mouth sensitivity
- skin sensitivity
- eye sensitivity
- allergies

In the Workplace/Hobby

- does not like warm or hot environment (room temperature – sunning – tanning)

6. Long labor   (over several days)

Manifestations in Later Life

Mental/Physical

- slowness of body movement
- slowness relating thought to word and word to action
- stress

In the Workplace/Hobby

- slowness in decision making
- fights to win and does

7. Too much anesthesia   (up to and sometimes including overdosing)
Manifestations in Later Life
Mental/Physical
  • sensitive to medical smells
In the Workplace/Hobby
  • attracted to the medical profession, medical science, or medical volunteer work (Red Cross, etc.)

8. Fetal distress   (near drowning in blood or body fluid)
Manifestations in Later Life
Mental/Physical
  • slow learner
  • dyslexia
  • breathing problems
  • stress
  • fear of blood
In the Workplace/Hobby
  • attracted to stress situations
  • attracted to color red or anything reddish

9. Caesarean section
Manifestations in Later Life
Mental/Physical
  • same as in **born too late**
  • or, if prematurely born, same as in **born too soon**
In the Workplace/Hobby
  • see #2 for born too late
  • see #1 for born too soon

10. Sound   (Sounds, e.g., music to womb via abdomen or after birth, while asleep)
Manifestations in Later Life
Mental/Physical
  • speech problem
  • autism
  • heart(beat) irregularities
  • relaxation dysfunctions
  • stress dysfunctions
  • compulsive yawning
  • supersensitive hearing
In the Workplace/Hobby
  • stress attitude towards sound, music and/or rhythm

* needs sounds to fall asleep by
* seeks out music (sounds) to escape from problems/stress
* attracted to anything having to do with sound, music or rhythm

Not included are the results of ultrasounds during pregnancy. Serious medical complications may occur in later life.

11. Pre-natal stress   (of the mother)
Manifestations in Later Life
Mental/Physical
* too strong a heartbeat
* sensitive to chest pains
* sensitive to throat irritation
* hyper-nervousness
* profuse sweating
* cold and wet hands
* nausea
* unspecified fears

In the Workplace/Hobby
* in constant search of stress situations
* always under stress
* fights the system and the workplace
* runs away from the system

12. Cold delivery   (room temperature)
Manifestations in Later Life
Mental/Physical
* feels generally cold
* one part of body feels cold, the part that sensed the cold in the birth process, e.g., the buttocks
* teeth clenching

In the Workplace/Hobby
* likes to be in warm places (inside) or in the sunshine (when outside)

13. Wrong feeding   (after birth, breast or bottle)
Manifestations in Later Life
Mental/Physical
* strong desire for milk
* strong dislike for milk
* likes sour fluids or solids
* needs to drink

- needs to eat
- needs to smoke
- teeth grinding
- allergies
- all-consuming kisses

In the Workplace/Hobby
- over-eating
- over-drinking
- smoking
- eating – drinking – smoking hobbies, e.g., gourmet cooking
- attracted to professions having to do with eating or food, e.g., nutritionist – dietitian – cook – chef – food buyer – diet freak

14. One live twin   (twins, of which one died in the womb, or in the birth process or soon thereafter, even if not known to have existed)

Manifestations in Later Life

Mental/Physical
- feels that "something" is missing
- searches for that "something" most of his life ("something" may include a person)

In the Workplace/Hobby
- always looks for or wishes for a "brother" or a "sister" type of person or a work or business partner of either sex

15. First time eyes are opened   (at or after birth while body is in motion)

Manifestations in Later Life

Mental/Physical
- vertigo
- fear of heights

In the Workplace/Hobby
- fear of flying
- fear of elevators
- fear of amusement rides
- fear of looking down from any elevation

16. Forced birth   (by hands or forceps)

Manifestations in Later Life

Mental/Physical
- intermittent pain at shoulder or any other place where pressure was applied
- concern about pain, not knowing cause

In the Workplace/Hobby
* concern about not being able to use certain muscles if needed for work or play

Please note: *Not* included in this study are the effects in later life of in-vitro fertilization and embryo transplantation, both occurring in *light*, rather than in their natural environment: *darkness*.

This *may*, and I emphasize *may*, result in physical or pathological problems or dysfunctions of organs in adult life.

Only time will tell ...

Instructions

SpM II is a simple procedure to overcome birth traumas and thus get rid of their associated manifestations in later life.

It can be done between two people, one willing to help (The Helper) and the other willing to be helped (The Subject). It can be done between two partners or even between parent and child. As a matter of fact, it is so simple that almost anyone can help another person who happens to have this kind of problem.

Now, come with me and listen to the lullaby of bearing

Heed specifically warnings #2 and #3 on page 29 and 30. Follow *to the letter* instructions, warnings and observations (pages 39 through 44), including the 23 steps. Only then continue as outlined below.

General Test

The following is the *first* thing the helper has to do in *all* types of birth trauma exercises. It is the foundation exercise from which subsequent ones take off. This one is to check if there *is* a birth trauma at all. If your subject does *not* react according to the following descriptions, there was *no* birth trauma!

First

* Your subject is on the bed, blindfolded.
* Tell him to turn onto his side. (*Don't* mention left or right side. If he asks you, tell him to turn onto the side which feels most comfortable.)

- You pull up his knees as close to his chin as they will go. At the same time, you put both his arms around his legs, just below his knees.
- Move his head forward, so that the top of his head is almost even with his bent knees.
- He now lies in an almost typical womb position.

Then

Hold your one hand against the back of his head and your other hand against his knees. Don't exert pressure. Tell your subject: "In your fantasy you are now in your mother's womb. Tell me what you feel." If he feels nothing, even sort of good, give him the following instruction: "When I count to three, jump out of the womb by rolling onto your back, stretching your arms and your legs at the same time."

"One . . . two . . . three." On the count of *three*, you pull off his mask and say in a commanding voice: "Open your eyes, breathe in deeply." (Be careful not to scratch his face with your nails when you lift off his mask.)

Put the tissue and the mask back on his eyes and do the same thing all over again. Observe his reactions. If you are satisfied that there are no negative reactions—meaning no fear, no uncomfortable feeling, no difficulty in breathing, no sweating . . . instead it all feels sort of good—you may end this session.

Help him to sit on the edge of the bed.

A subject who has *no* birth trauma will *not* react to this exercise, whatever you try and no matter how many times you try it.

However, if, at the moment the subject is lying on his side in his womb position and he starts to feel nervous, feels stress or has fears, starts to sweat, get cold, or his heart start to palpitate, he has had a birth trauma. Do the same exercise but observe if your subject, immediately *after* he jumps out of the womb, feels a tremendous *relief.* If he does, he *does* have a birth trauma.

During the exercise let him do all the reacting he wants to do and wait till his reactions have finished. Then tell him to go back to the womb position, wait for his symptoms to come back (that may take a little time), count to three and let him jump again. Repeat as often as necessary until there is absolutely no nervousness (or other symptom) left while he is in the womb position. You may have to repeat the exercise from three to eight times, occasionally a few more times.

If there are *strong* reactions, it is a good idea to check his birth the next day again, even though it seems to have worked out completely the day before.

Back to the Tunnel

General exercise #2, to be done immediately after the helper has finished the general test.

The subject is still on the bed and blindfolded in the womb position. The helper tells his subject: "In your fantasy, you are inside a tunnel and at the end of the tunnel you see a light. Tell me what the tunnel looks like and feels like and how bright or dim the light is at the end of the tunnel." Your aim is to get him to go to that light and into the "day." These are symbols for birth canal and room (or day) light.

Tell him to move towards the light through the wet tunnel. Some subjects use another name, like sewer. Use your subject's word, not your own. Sometimes the tunnel is dry and the subject may get an itchy or burning feeling on his skin. That's OK. It's all a repetition of the trauma he underwent during his birth. As you should know by now, all we want to do is pull information hidden in the subconsciousness to the surface, into the consciousness.

We go on. The helper says: "When I count to *three*, you're out of the tunnel and you turn onto your back. *One... two... three*." On the count of *three*, take off his eye mask and say: "Open your eyes (which will be very difficult for your subject) and look around." Then put the blindfold back on. Repeat this exercise as often as necessary until it becomes meaningless to the subject. In order to find out *when* this occurs, you will ask for his reaction after each time you take off his mask. Eventually the helper will notice the sincerity of his subject's feeling of superfluousness. These two exercises are for the simplest birth traumas, without much complication in adult life if any at all.

Exercise "Born Too Soon"

Born too soon can range from a seven months premature baby to a baby who was born "exactly" on time. The doctor, the mother and whoever else who was involved in establishing the "exact" birth date may have all agreed that the baby was "on time." However, the baby himself might have had other ideas. He wasn't ready yet. He was having a good time in his mother's womb and really enjoying his euphoric state. It was a nasty experience to be pushed out of the womb into the cold and into the bright light. He'd much rather have stayed cuddled up in his warm and protected "house."

People who have gone through this experience during the birth process do have, in their adult life, a tendency to "crawl back into the womb." Translated into day-to-day life, that means: Sleep often, go to bed early, have difficulty getting out of bed in the morning, and go to bed when confronted with problems. They are often tired without any good reason. They may give up easily on the things they had planned to do and they may not start things (plans, projects) that they know will require much effort.

The following exercise will get them out of these habits: Tell your subject to go into the womb position. Tell him that he *is* in the womb and that it is very comfortable there. Let him thoroughly enjoy his comfort. Then tell him that it is time to be born. Suggest to him that he doesn't want to yet. Then suggest again that it is so comfortable, while also suggesting that there is pressure to get out of the womb.

Ask him: "Do you really want to get out?" Of course he says: "No." So, you make a deal with him: "How many more days do you want to stay in?" He may answer: "15." "OK" you say, "I will count to 15 and then you come out." You count out loud backwards from 15 to 1: "15 days . . . 14 more days . . . still 13 days . . ." etc., down to: "one more day."

After you have reached one, you put him slowly on his back, take his mask off, very gently, tell him to open his eyes and make him feel good by saying, for instance: "Well, doesn't that feel good?"

You're now going to repeat the same exercise. This time, however, your subject may say that he wants to stay in only 11 more days. Count from 11 down to 1. You continue the exercise until he is down to "1 more day." Then, change to hours: "How many more hours (of that one last day) do you want to stay in?" Keep going with this exercise, each time with a countdown, on his back, mask off and some encouraging words, until the whole thing becomes meaningless to him and he just doesn't feel the need any longer to stay in his mother's womb.

Exercise "Born Too Late"

The doctor, the mother, and whoever else was involved in establishing the "exact" birth date may have all agreed that the baby was "on time." However, the baby himself might have had other ideas. He was ready perhaps a day or so before that time, or it could be just hours earlier. His mother may also have taken too much time with him (long labor), at least as far as he was concerned.

In such a case, the baby starts to work his way out of his mother's womb, but has a heck of a time. His brain keeps sending messages to his muscles but all the baby's efforts are to no avail yet. The stress in these specific muscles that were activated by the brain, that he used (while still in the womb), may remain tense for the rest of his life, beginning at age 16.

In later life, he will sometimes start things (plans, projects) but will give up easily, pronouncing it (the project, etc.) to be a "prayer without end" or he will mark his project as "being useless." Yet, he will start the same thing or perhaps a similar project all over again. Eventually, he most probably will succeed. There is this other possibility when— under the same circumstances as mentioned above—the baby is not using its muscles, even though he is ready to be born. He is just w-a-i-t-i-n-g and w-a-i-t-i-n-g – This birth trauma may produce, in his later life, a slowness of body movements, a slowness of thought to words and words to action, and a slowness in decision making.

The following exercise will get rid of the stress feeling in your subject's muscles. Put your subject in the womb position. This time, helper, put your one hand on the back of his head and your other hand below his knees. If your hand is not big enough, hold your hand *and* underarm across (just below) his knees. Start applying pressure, bringing his head and knees together. Push, first gently, then with more force. Tell your subject to jump out of the womb. Because of the pressure on the head and knees, it will be difficult for your subject to "jump." Now, your pressure is going to change into strength and you really have to hold him tightly. Say: "When I count to three, you free yourself and jump out of the womb. *One . . . two . . . three.*" At the count of *three*, you let your hands go and at the same time pull the mask from his eyes. Tell him to immediately open his eyes, look around and relax. "Breathe in deeply and relax."

Because the position in which you had to hold your subject was awkward—you had to bend over and, at the same time, exert pressure—you may now tell your subject to lie on his back, pull up his knees towards his face, and put his arms around his shins. In this way, your position becomes easier because you only have to put pressure on his hands and shins, and no longer on his head. Keep repeating the exercise until there are no more reactions and then try again.

Next phase of the same exercise: At your count of *three*, your subject thinks that he can jump out again, but this time you apply all the strength you have on top of his shins so that he can't jump. Hold him until his strength overtakes your pressure. (The subject has more strength in his legs that you have in your arms.) Then let go suddenly. Pull off the subject's mask, and tell him to open his eyes, breathe in deeply and relax. Repeat, repeat, repeat.

Final phase of the same exercises: We are now going to use and play the "unexpected" game. You build up something by saying, for instance, "One . . . two . . . three" and *not* doing what the subject expects at three but doing it between one and two. He will get confused. This confusion is necessary to make your subject arrive at a concept of reality. After all, the purpose of these sessions and the whole SpeyerMethod is to draw back blocked information from the subconscious to the conscious. Continue until his strength has disappeared. Note: This "unexpected" game should be played with all exercises where counting is indicated, throughout all of SpeyerMethod II.

Breech Birth . . . and Phillip

A breech baby is born upside down, breeches first instead of head first. During this process, it may happen that the fluid from the mother's womb runs along the baby's face giving a sensation of drowning and suffocating.

The case history of Phillip is a simple illustration of how a *latent* birth trauma can become active through one particular set of life's circumstances. Phillip worked on a small ocean freighter. He was happy with his life, his wife, his children and his work, Everybody liked him. One day, the freighter collided with another ship and sank. He saved his life by climbing through a short, narrow chimney that ran from the galley to the upper deck. While climbing out, seawater poured down the chimney, almost drowning him, cutting off the air supply. He nearly suffocated but made it to the deck and was saved. All the others on board drowned. When he came to see me he had been treated for the previous two years for what was thought to be a "guilt complex." During those two years, he had not been able to work and had lost interest in life, wife and children. The so-called guilt feeling was supposedly based on the fact that he was the only survivor and that he felt responsible for (or guilty about) the death of his shipmates. That had been the opinion of a number of psychiatrists (at a University clinic) who had treated him over a two year period without any result. During SpeyerTherapy, I discovered that he had been a breech baby. Chances are he might not have suffered from his birth trauma during his entire life, never knowing about this particular aspect of his birth. However, the near-drowning experience that Phillip had, which was an almost perfect repetition of his breech birth, started a cycle of depressions, mistakenly labelled as "guilt." By bringing Phillip's deeply hidden trauma to the surface (to his consciousness), the problem disappeared.

Exercise: Subject lies on his back, blindfolded. You suggest that he is going to re-live his birth. Wet your hands and spread your wet fingers as wide as possible. Slide your wet fingers along the subject's face from the top of his head, across his hair, forehead, cheeks, nose, lips, and chin toward his throat. Then reverse the direction. Suggest to your subject that he feels water flowing past his face. Tell him to react by pushing away your hand, wrist, or underarm. Tell him to push hard. After each push, put your hand back on his face, all the time encouraging him to express his anger and/or fear.

Then say: "Keep pushing away the water until you feel that it is my hand and not longer water." In all exercises you must always put an *end* to aim for, in front of your subject. [Instead of, or in addition to, your wet fingers, you may also use a water-soaked towel.) End the exercise when the subject indicates he is consciously aware of what you are doing and has lost his fears.

Exercise for Navel String Birth

Your subject lies on the bed, blindfolded, relaxed. The helper has to stretch his (her) thumb and fingers in half-moon fashion and lay his hand around the subject's throat, imitating the navel string. He will push away your hand or grab with his fingers between your hand and his throat, pulling your hand away from his skin. Give the subject resistance. If his breathing starts to become difficult, which usually happens, take off his mask and tell him to open his eyes and look around the room, breathing in deeply. Keep doing this until the subject comes to a point where he likes the feel of your hand on his throat or until it has become meaningless. Test by touching the throat again and again, until it no longer affects his breathing.

Pre-Natal Stress ... and John

During the last couple of months of Mrs. Luke's pregnancy with her son John, she went through some nasty emotional experiences* and actually lived under constant stress. John is now 32. Since

---

*In general, such circumstances are: Unwanted pregnancy, marital problems, war, strong fears, fear of undue termination of the pregnancy, family, social, financial problems, etc.

the age of 16, he had constantly suffered uncomfortable and scary feelings, such as a strong heartbeat, feeling the unnatural pounding in his chest and throat, an undetermined, unspecified feeling of fear, hypernervousness, profuse sweating, cold and wet hands, and nausea. As so many like him, John had gone through 16 years of Valium and whatever else the various psychiatrists he visited saw fit to feed him. None of these specialists ever asked him questions about the emotional well-being of his mother during her pregnancy or even asked him any questions about his birth.

John: The Case of the Mother's Pre-natal Stress

While in my office, I explained to John: "You have in your body two glands which are located on top of your kidneys, They are called the adrenal glands. If you and your body are in any state of emergency, such as when your life is in danger, these glands see to it that you are either strong enough to fight off the danger or strong enough to go on a "flight," that is to flee from the danger. Hence, the expression when talking about adrenals, "fight-or-flight." The adrenal glands secrete certain hormones in your bloodstream that make your body extra strong on a moment's notice and keep it extra strong for as long as necessary. In other words, the normal sequence of operating is:

1. *Danger*	Information coming through the senses or from inside the body	
2. *Adrenals*	Start secreting immediately	
3. *Fight or flight*	Extra strength to cope	

In John's case, however, we have a different situation. In his fetal status, John's adrenal glands observed a continuous stress (danger) signal. This signal came from the stress his mother was experiencing. John's adrenal glands reacted and stress (danger) became their norm.

The real and general norm for these glands is, of course, a relaxed state. The not-so-normal norm, stress, starts to become apparent in later life during the middle or late teen years, usually around 16, sixteen! The adrenals then perform the following sequence:

1.	*Adrenals*	Work all the time
2.	*Fight or flight*	Extra strength, feels like stress
3.	*Danger*	Which, in reality, isn't there

John (and, of course, anybody else under the same circumstances) is now searching for difficult circumstances to satisfy fight or flight feelings. He is living, therefore, under constant stress. Stress and the search for stress have become his norm. His entire adrenal system is reversed.

Exercises for Pre-Natal-Stress

The following four exercises must be done in sequence, one after the other, without interruptions.

1. I told John to lie down on the bed and turn onto his side, left or right, whichever felt more comfortable, more natural. He chose his left side. He was blindfolded, his knees pulled up against his chest, arms around his legs. I told him to imagine himself inside his mother's womb and to feel strongly his mother's stress and nervousness. "Feel your own fears, John. Feel your heartbeat, feel your cold hands, feel how you take over her nervousness."

    "Now, when I count to three, jump out of your mother's womb, throw out your arms and your legs, look around, breathe in deeply and relax. OK, here we go (and I count very slowly) *one . . . two . . . three.*" At this point, John jerked onto his back, throwing out his arms and his legs. At the very same time I pulled the mask from his eyes, pulling the trauma into reality, into consciousness. He breathed in deeply, relaxed and his stress symptoms faded slowly away.

    I repeated the same exercise several times until it became difficult for John to get his stress feeling back while he was in "his mother's womb."

2. Then, I told John to lie on his back and feel the same stress again. "When I count to three, the stress feeling will disappear." This time, he did not have to make all those movements. It just became a routine exercise to feel alternatively stressed and relaxed.

3. John is lying on his back blindfolded. I put my fingers on that part of his back where his adrenals are located, just above the

kidneys. "When I press, you feel stress . . . when I let go, you relax." Do this a few times and then: "And now rhythmically, John, feel stress (finger on) . . . two . . . three . . . four, relax (finger off) . . . two . . . three . . . four." This, too, is repeated several times.

4. "Imagine, John, that the two adrenals look like fire hydrants or big faucets. In your fantasy you make yourself as little as a match. Walk around in your body and look at these faucets. First, you *open* the faucets and feel the hormones flow into your bloodstream. You will feel stress moving throughout your body. Now, turn off those faucets. Feel the muscles of your hand while doing this. Work slowly and feel the stress flow stop. Relax"

The flowing away of the stress will take a few moments, sometimes up to half a minute.

We repeated this several times until he found a conscious control system with which to operate, even when he is not in my office. After a while, this will no longer be necessary because the symptoms will have disappeared. The adrenals will have been reversed to their original biological norm.

Exceptions

Those who have been affected by years of psychodrugs, strong chemical inhibitors and the like will have problems. A chemical wall (threshold) has been built between the subconscious and the conscious. The necessary communication between the two cannot be properly effected by SpeyerMethods. These people should see an endocrinologist.

Sureties and Securities in All Cases

- Your subject must *become aware* of his alternative feelings of true stress and his fear of it.
- The helper must make sure that during the course of the sessions his (her) subject gets *fully involved* in his feeling of stress and just as fully involved in his feeling of relaxation.
- After all the exercises, *talk together* about subject's reactions.
- Whatever happens, once you have started the SpeyerMethod, you *must finish*, regardless of how long it takes.

Feeding the Baby

Although feeding the baby is not really connected with birth traumas, it is so close to it, that this seems to be the right moment to mention what can go wrong if, for instance, the mother is not on time to feed her baby, not interested, too nervous, too preoccupied with other things, too impatient, or is under- or over-feeding her baby.

If your mother "practiced" any of the above some results later in life may be: Strong like or dislike for milk or other specific fluids, foods, or tastes, the need to drink or eat all the time, the need to smoke, the need to "suck."

Exercise

Subject lies on his (her) back, blindfolded. Tell him to take his thumb and put it in his mouth and *not* to touch it *with his teeth.* Let your subject decide whether to take his right or left thumb. Tell him to start sucking his thumb and imagine that he is really sucking his mother's nipple when he was a baby. If the subject claims, at this point, that he was bottle fed, tell him that this doesn't make any difference. Let him have his own thoughts for a while. Make sure that your subject is really in there and loving every moment of it.

In the meantime, bring your hand under the subject's wrist. Make sure *not to touch* his underarm or anywhere else. He must not know or feel the whereabouts of your hand. Then, with a sudden swing, pull his thumb out of his mouth. This will give your subject a terrible shock. He may start crying and/or cursing at his mother. Let him do that, let him even fight with her. Then put his thumb back in his mouth and repeat and repeat until the whole thing becomes meaningless to your subject and there are no more reactions.

Second Step Take your (blindfolded) subject and move his body straight up until he sits on the edge of the bed, facing you. Keep the mask *on.* Put a towel around his neck, covering the chest area. Put an empty pail on his lap. Take a bottle filled with water (room temperature) and let him drink. Again, tell the subject that, in his fantasy, he is sucking his mother's breast. When he is pleasantly involved in sucking water from the bottle, you suddenly pull the bottle away from him. That, too, will be a shock. However, this time there will not be further reactions. Repeat this until it becomes meaningless to your subject.

Last Step Finally, give your subject the bottle again. Make sure that it is full of water. Make the subject drink till the water "comes out of his ears," and then some more.

Observe all information
pertaining to the three months
digestion/adaptation period
Read: *"After the sessions are over"*
pages 49 through 52
Hosanna and Hallelujah and T.G.I.F.
but not yet

The Womb, Birthplace of the Human Race

The womb is the birthplace of the human race. Nature has given the embryo and the fetus the opportunity to develop in a perfect setting. The status of the unborn being is one of perfection, of utmost well-being, of euphoria. In the womb is security, warmth, protection. It is almost pure quietness.

After one point, however, the unborn baby can hear the voice of his (her) mother. But he only hears the *sound* of her voice, not her words. These sounds are like "maom, maha, muha, muom" and the like. Hence, the origin of baby's first word: "Mama" or "Mom" or "Mommy," all meaning Mother. In almost *all* languages the word "mother" contains the letter "M." They were the first sounds an unborn child got to "know" and they registered in his brain.

Many forms of meditation use certain words representing a sound (sometimes called a mantra). These meditation sounds bring you back into a euphoric state, reminding you of your stay in your mother's womb. The purpose of these words, or sometimes monotone chanting (as in some churches), is to bring you back to the relaxed state that your subconscious mind still remembers. It's a sliding back into wombmemory.

A Letter from Connie

A Letter About an End That Turned into a Beginning

Dear Simon,

Of course, you may use my letter for your book. Your method did wonders for me. So much so, that I can't stand to be alone anymore.

It's hardly possible for me to realize now what sort of scared little girl I was. I want you to use my case because, if it would only help one other little girl, I have done my part.

I would beg all Mommies and Daddies to learn from my story and beg them to, please, love their little girls.

When I was little, I always felt so lonely, so cold and so scared. Do you know what it means for a little girl who has no place to go? How often did I dream about and wished that my Daddy just said one word to me or just maybe ... touch me ... that wasn't asking too much, was it ... ? I wanted to cry oh, so softly and beg, yes beg ... please Daddy, love me ... please Mommie, love me ... please ... just love me ... please ... ?

•

•

•

Heed All the Warnings ...... Again!

From page 2, IZ accentuates how one single letter can influence an entire sentence. But, above all, it signifies that there is no such thing as perfection. Yet, one letter (... or is it one man?) can make a difference.

Chapter Six

SOME PHILOSOPHICAL, ANECDOTAL AND PROGNOSTIC VIEWS ABOUT THE SPEYERMETHODS®

The Speyer Method Helping to Overcome Stress

Like all psycho-biological symptoms, stress is really an extremely simple phenomenon. The simplicity, of course, became obvious only after years and years of deep thinking and a great deal of research, but isn't that always the case with everything?

Stress is "located" in the electrical/chemical make-up of our brain (i.e., for the purpose of this book; there is also such a thing as physical stress, in cases of illness or accident).

The origin of stress lies within the scope of our brain's energy Input-Storage-Output System.

Input: Information received through our senses;
Note: There are other inputs, such as from within the body (e.g., a latent illness), from the paranormal (e.g., intuition) or from a pre-natal birth trauma;
Output: The use and expression of *input* information;
Storage: In between input and output lies the information storage. Other labels for this arsenal of living and working information are: Processing, incubation, and digestion.

According to certain universal laws, output should always be more or less equal to input. Example: You hear a joke (input) ... you process the joke (storage) ... you laugh (output).

Now, imagine that you hear a very funny joke but, this time, you are *not allowed* to laugh! There is plenty of input but *no* output. This will create a temporary feeling of stress. This joke is, of course, a very simple illustration which really doesn't matter much in the long run. It will not cause any permanent stress.

But, imagine that this input-and-no-output is happening during your entire lifetime, every day and in all kinds of situations. It could be because of family pressure, or having to maintain and improve your status in the workplace, or perhaps because of social or political situations. In that case, you've got a serious problem. And this in addition to input-never-turned-output fear of parents, which is still lingering in the subconscious.

All this is lodged in your brain, waiting to be turned into output. In the meantime, it has spoiled the quality of your life for a good many years.

Note: Some other stress situations do not become active until the age of 16 or at menopause, or when there is a great loss of resistance, or when unknowingly repeating a birth or childhood trauma.

How does one get rid of this excess brain energy and consequently of stress? One has to go back to the *original* input information, which still lies in storage, and turn *it* into output! The key to the solution is *the original information*. Let's illustrate this with a case:

1. Harry is experiencing stress, caused by his boss.
2. I tell him to go play tennis, hit a baseball, or do some boxing or karate, as long as he has an imaginary or real opponent. Every time he hits the ball, he must think that it is his boss instead of the ball. In this way, he can get rid of his stress.
3. That evening, Harry really feels great but, unfortunately, stress re-appears after a couple of days.
4. So, *that* didn't work!

Next:

1. This time, I tell Harry to go and play tennis (or whatever else)
2. "But, every time you hit the ball, you think it's your father's (and *not* the boss') head, instead of the ball."
3. He will now get rid of his stress, related to his boss, for good.

This tournament, of course, is an enormous oversimplification of matters. But the core, the essence, of this example holds indeed the key to any stress cure. In this particular case, Harry's boss represents a subconscious memory of his father. Needless to say, the same goes for a female boss and mother.

In order to get rid of any stress, you must go back to the original input which still lies in storage, activate it, and turn it into output. Make sure, however, to direct your efforts to the original person and not to a look- or act-alike, such as your boss instead of your father.

If you are capable of discovering the core of your own stress (they used to call that Freudian psychoanalysis), then start a daily routine this way:

1. Close your eyes.
2. In your fantasy, hit that "original person" with your fists (or hands or feet or bite him/her or all) using a pillow, think it's *him* (or *her*).
3. Say or scream out loud whatever anger comes to your mind and direct your emotions to the *original culprit*.
4. Always say out loud *his* or *her name* (Father, Dad, Mother, Mom).
5. Continue this as a 5-day-a-week, 10 to 20 minutes a day routine or until this whole procedure becomes meaningless and whatever you try, no more anger can be produced.
6. When, at a later date, your stress shows its ugly head again, start all over. It's just like taking an aspirin for a headache.
7. If you can't find the original culprit who caused your stress, go to page 177 "Who Am I?," and to Getting to Know You #1 and #2 respectively on pages 179 and 189 and find out by playing the games.

The SpeyerMethod and the Male

Males who have gone through the SpeyerMethod, have literally grown taller, varying from ⅛ to ¾ of an inch. Women's breasts will get a little firmer or larger. (This also happens in a number of psychotherapies.) How is this possible? The genetic-biological energy, which was originally intended to be used to make one a "fully grown" person, was instead detoured and used to nourish one's hangups. In other words, it became an energy-wasting machine that didn't know what to do with itself.

As a result of doing the SpeyerMethod, this energy is diverted back into its originally intended genetic growth process.

All this sounds very interesting but even more interesting is that this body-energy wasting machine is, at the same time, connected to the *emotional* energy-wasting machine . . . to compulsive thoughts, behavior and actions . . . to hang-ups.

Here, too, a growth process—very much more important than the one which made you grow an inch—is apparent. Something else is happening. The road "to the top" has been cleared. Time and time again it appears that males, after having done SpeyerMethod, have been given promotions or have chosen another profession better suited to their own personalities, life-styles, or characters. How was it possible that these men never reached their full potential in the workplace?

In order to fully understand this, you will have to accept the principle of programming by parents in early childhood—(0–3½)—as described in Chapter One "Why Do I Do What I Do?"

If for instance, a father continually criticizes his son, continually degrades him, makes him fearful of expressing himself, indicates to his son that he will never amount to anything, that he can never do anything right, the son's and later the adult male's program and guidance mechanism will read: "I am worthless." And with this to-himself-unknown guidance system, he will indeed never amount to anything, never accomplish anything of real value, never get the promotion he deserves, and all this in spite of his potential. By doing the SpeyerMethod, he will lose his "I am worthless" complex and can develop according to his real, intended Self.

There are many men, however, who in spite of their hang-ups—or perhaps just because of them—do reach the top. With few exceptions, these men have also many serious health problems, have high blood pressure or suffer heart ailments or other so-called manager's illnesses, become alcoholics, or possibly develop cancer. In the workplace such a man appears to be destructive and, as a result of his often irrational projections, he is frequently in some sort of conflict situation. I would bet that you know who I am talking about.

After the SpeyerMethod, these men will finally develop a more relaxed attitude (after how many years???) and an ease of mind they had always searched for but never found. Their capabilities will remain as they were, their insight will expand, they will have more time for their families and hobbies . . . their quality of life will be considerably enriched.

Then, there is another category of men. They do *not* make promotion after the SpeyerMethod. They—again genetically speaking—do not possess the urge and/or capabilities to "climb to the top." They are finally satisfied that they don't have to "achieve" any longer. They will find another way of life, geared toward their own real Self, and they will be happier because of it.

The SpeyerMethod and the Female

From Adam and Eve up to and including the present "Mr. & Mrs.," the man came and still does come first.

The raw reality of this symbolism, which has its inception in the Judeo-Christian Bibles, is that it was the woman who revealed (forbidden) knowledge. She had to pay dearly. She had to pay a horrible price for her "crime." All she was ever good for was to be a sex object and to bear children. She was also required to be submissive to her male master, unto all eternity (freely after Genesis 3:16).

Biologically, and based on a male/female hormonal balance in the human body, this story could be supported: The woman, not the man, bears children. The man, not the woman, is physically stronger. Yet, behind every man there is a woman with her own subtle powers. In this way, man and woman, or woman and man (!) have always walked through life together, from the Garden of Eden into the Garden of Suburbia.

The biblical Queen of Sheba, who travelled to the court of King Solomon to convince herself of his wisdom and glory, used her sensuality and sexuality to be received by him (a feat which was apparently not very difficult, knowing Solomon). Out of their meeting, twin sons were born (freely after Kings 10:1–13 and after Ethiopian folklore).

After Adam's Eve, Solomon's Sheba, Samson's Delilah, Caesar's and Anthony's Cleopatra, and after who-knows-who's Marie Antoinette, in our time some truly emancipated women stood upright in this world as "men," without giving up either motherhood or femininity. I can think of Mme. Curie, Pearl Buck, Golda Meir, Mrs. Gandhi, and Margaret Thatcher, among numerous others. But, in spite of their emancipation, most women are still in a submissive, minority position, not only legally, but also in the family, in society, and in the workplace. Relationships and marriages are still ruled by men and men are still the main determinants within social, professional and business structures.

By using her sensuality and her sexual delights, the woman not only knew how to maintain her status in male society, but often took advantage of it and held important positions. To a lesser degree this holds true for a great number of women in this day and age. I know a woman who has sex with her landlord—for an hour or so a month—and thus pays her rent. She thinks nothing of it and is definitely not a prostitute. Nor is this an exceptional story. Be assured that, in essence, many male/female relationships still work that way.

Let me recount a real-life story of an elderly couple married for 40 years: A story about a wife who is afraid of her husband and is also afraid to express herself to him. Every morning at breakfast, Harry cut—almost ceremonially—the dark crusted heel of their fresh morning bread and gave it to his wife, Helen, who sat across the table from him. One morning, Helen suddenly took this morsel of bread and threw it back across the table at Harry. She accompanied the morsel with words of utmost desperation: "Harry, for forty years now, I didn't say anything. For forty years I ate that piece of bread against my liking.

For forty years I've hated every bite of it." Harry sat there, totally confused, mum. After a while, he uttered: "But, Helen, for 40 years, I did this for you, because I thought that you liked it so much. Just for one time, in all those years, I would have liked to eat it myself, I like it so much."

Non-communication comes in many forms . . .

After a woman has done the SpeyerMethod, we see, time and time again, that the now "liberated" woman is no longer afraid of her husband (lover) the way she had been afraid of her father. She doesn't have to be submissive any more if she doesn't want to be and doesn't need to fake a headache if she doesn't want sex.

The now-independent woman is going to do the things she always wanted to do but never dared because of her husband. She is going to play the piano or paint, play tennis or get involved in her hobbies. She is going back to school, takes courses, is going to look for a job, or goes into politics or business. She is more relaxed and, as a consequence, looks healthier and younger.

Because of her newfound independence, her relationship with her husband will change. If he still needs his "former" wife to nourish his neurosis and *he* didn't do the SpeyerMethod, then it is an excellent bet that the marriage will end. If he, too, did the SpeyerMethod, then they both have to work hard to develop a new relationship together and make it a success. Either that, or both should agree to end the marriage and stay friends as two people, rather than as male and female.

The woman can live without a partner, or do as she pleases and be happy with it.

The SpeyerMethod and the "Second" First Marriage

In parts of Africa and Asia bride and groom meet for the first time on the day of their wedding ceremony. Most of them see each other then for the first time in their lives. Their respective families, however, arranged this marriage years before, sometimes even before the children were born or just after birth. The price for the bride and other (usually financial) conditions and sometimes even divorce conditions are part of the pre-nuptial agreement.

One day, while doing research in Kenya in East Africa, I was invited to one of my African co-workers' wedding. I was flabbergasted when I received his invitation and said to him: ". . . but you've been married for years and you've got four children!" (This is a true story.) And he answered: "We never really officially got married because I have not been able to pay off my father-in-law. I had not yet completely paid for his daughter . . . until now." (The total price was 40 cows.)

So, too, is this a true story: A Pakistani husband and wife (Ismaelians of the Aga Khan's sect), were happily married for many years. They explained to me how a parents-chosen, pre-arranged marriage actually works.

They themselves were married according to this concept. First, the wife related her side of this type of marriage arrangement: "We saw each other for the first time on our wedding day. In the beginning my feelings for my husband were more of a duty nature, rather than of an emotional type of love. I knew it had to be this way; it had been for so many generations before me. I grew up in this system. I gave myself to my husband as a woman because it was my duty in life. I tried to excel, to be good to him, made delicious meals, kept the house in good order, served all his wishes at his slightest command, and satisfied him sexually."

Then he added: "In the beginning I, too, felt it more as a duty than anything else, but eventually I started to appreciate her taking care of me. I expressed these feelings to her, probably my first feelings of love. And, of course, that caused a reaction from her side, too. Because she felt my appreciation, she no longer felt it as a duty and started to love me too. And that's how we grew to love each other." (*Note*: Today, in Pakistan, a man and a woman may "refuse" three times a partner chosen by their parents. Divorces hardly ever happen, and when they do, it's almost exclusively among intellectuals.)

In our present-day Western Civilization, whether a couple lives together or separately, they have to get to know each other over an extended period of time before they commit themselves to one another. Then, after a number of years, divorce may loom. Sometimes this results in a legal separation, or sometimes—probably more often—the separation just happens quietly, and sometimes not so quietly, within the family. Now, I ask you, who is better off.

A great deal of fault, in our Western Society, must be placed at the door of our upbringing (programming). The more obvious, but not-so-often brought, reasons for divorce are:

1. One partner cannot communicate, the other can
2. One partner is affectionate, the other isn't
3. One partner has fear of spouse, the other doesn't understand this
4. One partner is insecure, the other is self-assured
5. One partner is compulsively aggressive, the other peaceful

In situations where each partner nourishes the other's hang-up, the sword is two-edged. In spite of the fact that one or both partners hate arguments, they create them.

How do we solve this problem?

Let's say that both partners went through the SpeyerMethod and let's also say that both of them got rid of their compulsive attitudes towards each other. Then what? Here are now two "new" people facing each other, two people who will have to live together as if they have known each other for years but, in reality, are now strangers to each other.

Looking once more at the Pakistani couple who didn't know each other when they got married, a Western couple could follow the same route as the Pakistanis did, especially considering the investment they have in each other in terms of children and time together. They now have to get to know each other all over again. They have to get used to the "new" old partner and if it takes a feeling of *duty*, by all means, try it! The marriage may be worth the "price of a cow," especially when you take that "cow" by the horns.

Am I a Father Figure, A Mother Figure, or What? . . . And Triggering

Being a "father" or a "mother" figure could happen to anyone in his or her life without even realizing that a relationship—individual, professional or in the workplace—is based on a subconscious parent-child—or vice versa, child-parent—early childhood situation. In other words, a father/mother figure situation can work in one of two opposite directions:

1. You can be a "father" or "mother" to someone else, usually a younger person, but not necessarily so
2. You can regard someone—usually an older person, but not necessarily so—as a "father" or "mother" figure

In both cases, "99 out of a 100 times," neither the "child" nor the "parent" is aware of the underlying base for this relationship. It all happens on a subconscious level.

Stanley

Stanley was the office manager of an international import and export company. During the past 12 years, he had run the office by himself and the only person he was responsible to was his boss, the owner.

Stanley was the boss's right-hand man and confidant. At one point, the business had grown so big that Richard, the boss, decided to open a second office in another state. This office became HQ and, Richard too, moved permanently, appointing in his place a new general manager, who then became Stanley's boss.

One day, the new manager reported that Stanley sort of rebelled against everything that went on in the office, something he had never done during the twelve years that he had worked for Richard. Worse than that, he had secretly given confidential business information to Richard's competitors. Richard had to let Stanley go.

What's behind this story? I'll tell you, but first read the following case.

Dorine

During the past twelve years, Dorine has worked as a dental hygienist in the office of Mel Humphrey, D.D.S. Working for such an extended period of time meant, without any doubt, that she was an excellent technician. Then, one day, Mrs. Rodgers came in to have her teeth cleaned. The next day, Mrs. Rodgers called in and complained about Dorine's work. She had even left a cotton strip in Mrs. Rodgers mouth. Dr. Humphrey checked it out and it appeared that Mrs. Rodgers was right. He discussed it with Dorine. They both were unable to find a reason for that unfortunate happening. Dorine got a second chance.

Is This My "Son" . . . Or What?

In Stanley's case, his boss, Richard, was a father figure to him. When he left Stanley behind and appointed another "father," Stanley's forgotten trauma became instantly activated. What was Stanley's trauma?

Stanley's father was a good and concerned parent. He and his wife, however, decided to get a divorce and soon thereafter Stanley got a stepfather who was not interested in him. Stanley felt deserted by his father and neglected by his stepfather. He had never reacted to his childhood misery until he took revenge on his "father," his boss, Richard, 35 years later.

Is This My "Daughter" . . . Or What?

Dorine's problem happened to be a case of sheer coincidence. Dorine never saw eye to eye with her mother very much. In her diverse relationships, which were mostly with men, her childhood trauma with her mother, however, had not interfered with the quality of her lifestyle, including the quality of her work.

In her work Dorine had dealt with many women with no difficulty. Then, what triggered the mistakes she made with Mrs. Rodgers? Dorine's mother was a perfectionist and, according to her mother, Dorine never did anything right. But that was not the main reason for Dorine's mistake. The "secret" here of (subconsciously) accepting Mrs. Rodgers as a "mother figure" was—believe it or not—a scar on the face of Mrs. Rodgers in the same place in which Dorine's mother had a scar. While working on her mouth, Dorine continually observed the scar and instantly reverted back to a (subconscious) mother-daughter memory which was full of criticism. So, in order to make that situation come true again, Dorine's brain instructed her to make mistakes in order to get Mom's love.

"Triggering" is the key to this so-called parent-child identification process and the consequent "child" or "parent" behavior in later life. A person may never—in his entire walk through life—have an opportunity to need, or to be, a father or a mother to someone else. Yet, by sheer coincidence, something, a forgotten childhood memory, may suddenly be activated and, all of a sudden, there's "Mom" or "Dad" again.

By realization—which is very difficult to obtain—one may rid him or herself from this "childish" behavior.

Relationships and the Wish Syndrome

Our brain works very mechanically. You put some information in it and it will keep on working with that same information, just like putting a program in a computer. So, why shouldn't relationships work mechanically, too? After all, they do take place in one's brain.

Boy meets girl, girl meets boy, employee meets boss, boss meets employee, it's all determined by programs directing our computer brain's relationship department. "Determined," in this case, means how the relationship develops from beginning to end.

Sometimes, one wishes for an end to a lousy relationship. But, somehow, that end doesn't seem to come. One hangs on in desperation, sometimes even accompanied by a depression.

On the other hand, there are situations where one wishes that the relationship would last forever, and, darn it, it breaks off against all reason. You can say that one had a relationship problem when it feels like the problem is repetitious in its deterioration process.

How *does* your brain guide you into blissful as well as into not-so-blissful relationships?   The human brain is born with a number of genetically built-in survival systems.   Most of them are already programmed at birth.   One of these survival mechanisms, however, is *waiting* to be programmed *after* birth.   Let's call this the "Relationship-Program."   "Relationship," because, in essence, relationships *are* a form of survival.

Who is putting this program in your brain?   It's the people around you, mostly your father and mother, but not necessarily so.   For programming purposes, it could be any person acting like a father or a mother figure.   Whoever is on the spot will do.   Even the lack of either a father or a mother figure will register on the program.   It puts an "empty" spot where this figure was supposed to be.

This process takes place from about three months before birth till about 3½ years of age.   After 3½ you work—for the rest of your life—with *that* relationship program.

The basic law of programming is:

1. All *men* in your later life (after 3½) that you love or have to respect *must* act and react just like your *father*.   At least, that's what you expect from those men (mostly without your knowing that you do).
2. All *women* in your later life (after 3½) that you love or have to respect *must* act and react just like your *mother*.   And again, that's what you expect from those women (mostly without your knowing that you do).

Based on this law, we have a number of possibilities for relationships in adult life.

1. The one we love or respect, acts and reacts just like Mom and Dad.   In this case, we have a more or less happy relationship.
2. The one we love and respect does *not* act and react like Mom and Dad.   In this case we have a more or less unhappy relationship.

It's all very Basic-Black-and-White, because *if* Mom and/or Dad happened to have been bad parents—at your age 0–3½—you will be "attracted" to "bad" partners in your love life as well as to "bad" superiors in the workplace.

In case of "bad" programming, one will *always* have the *wish* for a better situation, which, of course, never came about in childhood and therefore never comes about in later, adult, life.   If the wish for a better situation does come about, one will destroy the good situation or run away from it. Programming, good *and* bad, has got to get its way. After all, don't forget, it's survival!

The SpeyerMethod, the Critic, and the Fault-Finder

In the entire history of the world, every great personality has always been subjected to criticism. Even our forefathers in the Animal Kingdom had this problem—the hierarchy within the baboon colonies, for instance. But we don't have to go that far back. A sales manager in a New York department store, the foreman in a Detroit automobile plant, or the tax collecior in the county of Los Angeles, and all other executives are always subject to criticism. Between the early baboon and the contemporary executive are such figures as Moses, Jesus, Darwin, Einstein, and Churchill.

Why is it that everybody who has achieved some status in life always has to be criticized? And then mostly by "spectators?"

For a great part it has to do with the genetic psycho-biological make-up of our chromosomes. The majority of all people, 79%*—the silent majority—possess a chromosome structure that determines that this group is "static." Static, in this case, means that they cannot cope with radical changes or so-called progress. As a consequence, these static-chromosomatized people will fight, criticize, or find fault with anything that disturbs their balance, their status-quo. Great personalities usually have a searching kind of mind. They are dynamic and most of the time progressive. Here too, their state of mind is dictated by their chromosome structure (6% of all people are searchers).* They seem to disturb the moderate, the conservative, and the orthodox thinking people, the 79% noted above.

These moderates, the status-quo people, fight all changes they can't easily cope with with disbelief, and, of course, with criticism and fault-finding.

Criticism comes in various packages. It can only be appreciated or denied if one is capable of finding the critic's or fault-finder's point of departure.

1. Criticism, coming from honest considerations, usually forms an honest personal opinion. This type of criticism comes from a person who is *not* influenced by his own ego-wishes or his

---

*Ref.: John L. Karlsson, Ph.D., M.D., "The Biologic Basis of Schizophrenia." Charles C. Thomas publisher, Springfield, Ill. 1966 Chapter 10, pages 64–68.

own fantasies, not by ego-fear, not by his emotional, sexual or territorial self-urges, and not by a variety of other fears or insecurities.

This person's criticism is based on honest, intellectual, logical, rational, objective and healthy emotional considerations.

Yet, even this objective person is still caught in his own psychobiological makeup from which it is—at best—difficult to escape. Only a person who possesses the real freedom to search within himself, to find where his criticism comes from, can be regarded as a true critic. This type of criticism contributes to improvements and progress and those are the criteria of criticism.

2. Criticism can also come from unreal, egotistical, jealous, narrow-minded, sadistic and masochistic considerations.

This is, in actual fact, not criticism at all. Rather it is an expression of fear or insecurity or sometimes a conscious or unconscious need to be aggressive, denigrating, underhanded, or cynical. The word "criticism" is, in this case, a misnomer. Instead it is verbal abuse from a powerless and impotent being.

3. Finally, criticism can be based on early childhood programming. If a person possesses a "poisonous" tongue, then he or she is probably imitating one or both parents. If parents were continually criticizing each other, then offspring will do the same in later life. To be critical has become the norm. This form of criticism is a hang-up. Once one has done the SpeyerMethod, he or she can discover the core of their criticism and then use this knowledge to their own advantage and to the advantage of the world we live in.

The SpeyerMethod, the Dictator and the Tyrant

To get the proper insight into the phenomenon of the "dictator/tyrant," we first have to look at the concept of universal, cosmological space-energy. Perhaps you might find this a little farfetched. Don't worry, you'll see that it will eventually lead us right into what dictatorships really are.

Everything that is alive, everything that starts, develops, deteriorates, and ends, does this only because of space energy. We have given this thermodynamic system labels like entropy and cybernetics.

1. *Entropy:** No life system, no human brain, nothing whatsoever
   containing energy, can keep that energy forever. After a period
   of time our thinking brain cells have to lose this energy too . . .
   until death do us depart.

2. *Cybernetics:** a biological process which, through its guidance
   and correction (feedback) system maintains, strengthens, protects and defends the *norm* of human and *all* life. It does this
   in order to keep it in dynamic balance until its predetermined
   point of death.

The interaction between entropy and cybernetics endeavors to keep
a human being alive and healthy from conception until death. Just as
the life span of one human being is dictated by this entropy/cybernetic
system, so is the history of mankind regulated by these same phenomena. Here, too, a conception-birth-development-deterioration-death
cycle is observable. It's called: Evolution. The birth and development of our human race is observable through the development from
animal/man via emotional/man to rational/man.

In order for human societies to stay in healthy condition, they must
move between political-left and political-right. If one side gets too
strong, the other must win the next election or the next revolution. It
is all governed by a cosmological cybernetic feedback system. And now
we come to the Dictator and his dysfunction; dysfunction, because the
only way to keep a constant "right" or a constant "left" regime in place
is by *power.*

Fortunately for Mankind, the feedback system will sooner or later
see to it that the proper balance will be restored. It's a pity that it
sometimes has to last so long. The world has known many of this sort
of dictator. Stalin, Hitler, Mussolini, and Amin are still fresh in our
memory.

What we do not observe in history or is not even mentioned in the
local newspaper is the dictator at home, within the family or in the
workplace.

In his own way, he (it's usually a man, although some women know
how to be dictatorial as well) is just as bad as the infamous political
dictator, especially when it comes to his wife and children. Everyone
knows at least one person like this. He is the dictator and fault-finder
in his own little world. What he gets out of this is a feeling of power,

---

*In this frame, only where it pertains to human beings and human societies. Its scope,
of course, is universal.

often sadistic to boot, something he couldn't get anywhere else. In his social circles as well as at work, he is usually an insignificant little man. His dictatorial behavior has, in all probability, been programmed into his brain by his parents in his early childhood. Programming, though, sometimes works in funny ways. If the dictator's wife comes from a family in which her father, too, was a dictator, then she might be "very happy" with her dictator husband. It translates into some sort of "security" for her, although as in her early days, of course, it is security with misery. If, however, she did not have a dictatorial father, there will be a truly miserable situation at home. The dictator syndrome will be perpetuated from generation to generation. By doing SpeyerMethod one can break out of this vicious circle.

The SpeyerMethod, a Capitalistic CEO* and a Progressive Politician

Let me introduce you to a hypothetical well-to-do family, the Johnsons, consisting of a father, a mother, and their two sons. The father, like his father, is chairman and CEO of a shipping empire. Within the family, however, when it came to emotions, they were very poor.

During their early childhood years both sons, Charles and George, lived in their own little worlds. The small amount of contact that existed between the parents and their sons concentrated around material things and monetary subjects. Family talk was mostly about "things," never about feelings or concepts.

The Johnsons had wanted only one son. Their first born, Charles, was destined to become his father's successor in the family shipping business. One son, therefore, was enough. George, the second born, was an undesired and superfluous offspring.

Today, both sons are adults. Charles, indeed, became *the* man in his father's empire. He contributes greatly to the Republican Party and votes conservative.

George, on the other hand, is a top figure in a progressive political party. He is active within the leadership and organizes protest movements, for which he also writes inflammatory articles.

How it is possible that two brothers, born of the same father and mother, are so diametrically opposite to one another in their political views? Of course, we'll have to go back to their early childhood. George discovered soon that he was an unwanted child. He got the

---

*CEO, Chief Executive Officer.

brunt of that attitude, not only by neglect from his father and mother, but also from the attitude of his brother Charles. Within the family group, George just didn't exist. He didn't get any attention, neither emotional nor material. Charles was not only the favorite of his parents but indeed also of the nurse and the housekeeper. Ma, of course, didn't have much time for either son. Charles has continued the family tradition. He is rich and "right-wing." Next to his "cool" wife he has a "warm" mistress (compare cool mother and warm nurse).

George, on the other hand, is full of childhood neuroses because (1) he got no attention, (2) he was always put in last place, and (3) he got less candy and later less pocket money. George is typical in that he transferred his unexpressed aggression from *then* (childhood home environment) to *now*, into the political field. He fights the establishment (read: his parents) with biting sarcasms.

When a person has reached an important status in this life, he can hardly admit that this has happened because of his childhood trauma. Besides, who will point this out to him? Both Charles and George have surrounded themselves with people who admire them and protect them against any intrusion from the outside world.

I am sure that all of us who read this story will shake our heads in disbelief to see how early childhood traumas can influence one's economic as well as political life. Worse yet, both brothers (as in all similar cases) influence your and my life, possibly to the extent of our survival or death.

The SpeyerMethod® and Criminology

It is, to say the least, remarkable to see how Man, in Western as well as well as in Eastern societies, reacts—emotionally and rationally— with respect to 1. *physical* pain and illness, vis-à-vis 2. *mental* pain and mental illness.

1. A physical illness, from a simple headache to a bypass operation, is always regarded with empathy and sympathy by the fellow men of the sufferer. From archaic medicine men to the most advanced medical scientists, they are there to help promptly.
2. Not so for those who suffer mental pain or mental illness. In the past these unfortunates were jailed, tormented, ostracized or destroyed. They were always punished and, to a degree, it is the same today.

If you will accept as a fact that everyone who commits an antisocial act—from shoplifting to murder—is at that moment mentally unbalanced, then any crime would have to be regarded as a result of mental dysfunction or mental illness. As a consequence, therefore, everyone who ends up in prison has to be, to say the least, mentally unbalanced, before, during, and after his anti-social act. Yet, he is only going to be punished, seldom treated. Punishing and revenge is the basic philosophy of criminal law.

Within this frame, there is, of course, an essential difference between the physically and mentally ill.

In case of crime, there is always someone else involved, the victim whose territory has been invaded, violated, raped, or destroyed. This, however, is the second phase of a criminal act. The starting point of the crime, premeditated or impulsive, originates in the "sick" mind of the perpetrator.

And this is where society fails!

The judicial system punishes and takes revenge, which may be OK, depending on your philosophy. But what the system fails to do is to institute a compulsory, automatic treatment process for everyone who commits non-violent as well as violent crimes.

The solution to our crime problem is *not* more prisons, more judges or a better judicial system with a different set of priorities. The solution is to help the criminal be cured of his illness that *caused* the crime in the first place. That's where our tax money should go.

Problem! The average prisoner doesn't believe in psychology, let alone any form of therapy directly applied to himself. Because no therapy will work without motivation, the question remains how to get the inmate motivated to undergo some form of therapy and to do something about his problem.

To witness the chilling screams, the foaming anger and the gut suffering that come out of a person during therapy catharsis is a deeply moving experience for any observer. No one can escape these true human reactions. Automatically, the observer feels the same pain. He cries too, gets angry too. Even when he tries to keep it within himself, it hurts his insides.

The solution, therefore, is to let motivated inmates (there are always some) undergo the SpeyerMethod, while other unmotivated prisoners, men and women together, are obligated by law to sit and witness the release of anger and mental pain. By seeing SpeyerMethod in action, by participating in its human drama, and by the inescapable identification process that is set in motion, most of the others should eventually also be motivated to get this or some other kind of help.

Through the SpeyerMethod, derailed persons can be brought back into the mainstream of our society. This, in turn, will produce a healthier family life, better citizens and less crime. Exceptions are those who, because of their chromosome structure—such as an extra-Y chromosome or because of other mal- or dysfunctions of the brain—have murdered, raped or mutilated. These criminals should be subject to mandatory medical (endocrinological) treatments.

The SpeyerMethod® and Religion

Religion is an emotionally loaded subject, especially when something like the SpeyerMethod gets involved in it, but be assured, it will all end up on a very positive note. From our humanoid time on, the God-idea has been an integral and ceremonial part of our daily life. It is a beautiful and fascinating feeling to feel as one with one's universal father. And with this belief, we protect ourselves against anything we don't know (as yet). How we should deal with Belief and Ceremony has been proclaimed to the masses in a variety of ways, in different parts of the world, over different eras.

The original proclamation of God's Word came from individuals who were striving for betterment for their fellowmen. They were humanitarian ideologists who, often against "fire and brimstone," announced the omnipotence and omnipresence of their God-on-Earth. They dictated, at the same time, the ceremonial structure of "believing." As long as these Sons-of-God were in power, there was hope for a better life, free of pain, hunger, illness, and slavery.

Unfortunately, the words and acts of these original Saviors were misused and wrongly interpreted by most of their followers.

This is not going to be a philosophical dissertation. What I want to demonstrate here is that the idea of God's power is often used as a personal ego-power instrument by those who are proclaiming they act in "His Name." "God" becomes then a punishment tool and a threat. Consequently, it becomes difficult to distinguish the Real God from the human-created fear-god.

This fear method is still used within the family when children are threatened with a punishing god if they don't behave. But his "god" is nothing more than the bad ego of the parents and has nothing whatsoever to do with the Real God. A realization (through the SpeyerMethods) that a "bad" god was created by his father and mother will most likely produce an insight of what the Real God and its accompanying religious feelings really are.

After the parents-induced fear-god has been "killed," one will, hopefully, realize that *God* is just a very private interpretation of one's communication with the Universe.

The Speyermethod® as a Result of Jewish Thinking

The term "Jewish thinking" is, of course, very vague. Most Jewish thinking, which, by the way, is not limited to Jews alone, has as its core the interrelationships of single bits of information. If you know info-bit A and info-bit B, Jewish thinking immediately deduces from that, info-bit C. Once the Jewish thinker has $A + B + C$, he is on his way to 9 info-bits $(A + B + C)^3$, etc., etc. In other words, nothing is ever stagnant or dogmatic in Jewish thinking. There is always that "other" possibility to come up with.

The world should be grateful for Jewish thinking. It has given us the Bible, Christianity, Socialism, psychoanalysis and $E = mc^2$. It would be super-conceited to add the SpM to this list and yet, in reality, it came about in the very same manner. SpM uses interrelations of many disciplines: Physics, cosmology, biology, cytology, anthropology, and the neurosciences. It is the God-given sensitivity, called Jewish thinking, that made it possible to know *what* to discard, *where* to combine, *how* to combine, *where* to integrate, or *where* to fuse, *where* to be abundant, and *where* to be efficient.

That's why there is such a remarkable difference between Jewish and non-Jewish thinking. That's why only those, Jews and non-Jews alike, who think in the Jewish manner, make such good doctors, lawyers, businessmen, strategists, and scientists. Again, I have to emphasize that, although this method of Jewish thinking originated when biblical Rabbis were interpreting the Torah, it's definitely not limited to Jews alone.

SpM is a result of this type of thinking. It is definitely *not* so-called psychology. It came about along the Empirical Road and therefore it will not stop here but grow on, combining and combining more and more bits of information, ad infinitum . . . .

The Speyermethod® 10 Years from Now

In my introduction, I stated that the SpeyerMethods I and II are to be considered a very serious indictment of the Establishment of professors, teachers, and practitioners in the fields of clinical psychology and psychiatry and of all others who dabble in counseling. Indeed, about 90 years of disastrous dabbling, pills and prejudices have ruled and are still ruling this field. It will take all of ten years to have a SpeyerMethod person helping his "neighbor" go through the SpeyerMethod in every block of every city, town, or hamlet.

Insurance companies and government social service departments should be the first to come to this insight and prefer to finance a network of volunteer (nonprofessional) SpeyerMethod helpers rather than—as they do now—pay endless millions of dollars in huge fees to members of the just noted establishments.

Churches, cultural centers, sport schools, school systems, and prisons, as well as personnel/social departments of corporations, service organizations and government agencies could be instrumental in helping members, colleagues, and co-workers to get rid of their seemingly never ending hang-ups.

Finally, the judges and juries, statesmen, and the Congress will come to grips with reality. Appropriate laws and realistic priorities will then be instituted. And that will be the beginning of the breakthrough of the nineties and the end of all that was.

Brain Science in the Work Place (BW)^{sm}

A no-cost, volunteer, non-professional Mental Health System based on the SpeyerMethod®

Over a period of some forty-odd years I have researched, developed and practiced a basic, uncomplicated, no-nonsense and above all, effective psychotherapy. It is commonly known as "SpeyerTherapy" and, since the early 1970s, widely practiced in Europe.

It helps people who are affected with hang-ups, stress, and depression to gain back the quality of life they're entitled to by virtue of being born human.

Out of the SpeyerTherapy, I developed the two self-help methods, described in this book. As we have seen, it takes only minutes-a-day, over a very short period of time. It can be done, not only at home, but obviously also in the workplace (in a room set aside for this purpose). There, it should be available at no cost to the employee and executive alike.

BW^{sm}'s main targets are national and international conglomerates, governmental agencies as well as scientific, financial, insurance and educational institutions.

In order to accomplish this "Utopia," the following steps have to be taken: In the first instance, volunteer helpers should be recruited from within the Corporation. Management has to make volunteer personnel available, as need be, on a temporary basis. In addition, paid helpers such as retirees, senior citizens, the unemployed, teachers and nurses may be recruited from outside.

First, BW^{sm} will train these volunteers and helpers. At a later stage, out of these helpers, salaried instructors will be selected who will then become clones of the 'original' BW^{sm} helper and they can then start training more volunteers/helpers. Thus, BW^{sm} can be spread around the nation and, as a matter of fact, around the world.

Global Areas in Which BW^{sm} Can Be Applied

• In the workplace (see above);
• Teachers can be trained to teach children self- and family analysis, either in groups or individually, all on their own age level;
• Nurses can be trained to help their patients lessen stress and depression, but only if connected with their mental attitude toward their illness or because of adverse family circumstances. This program must be medically supervised.

In addition to the "run of the mill" problem person, the following categories of people could also benefit from BW^{sm}:

• World War II POWs, Holocaust survivors, and Vietnam veterans can do the SpeyerMethod in BW^{sm}'s context to alleviate or at least diminish the effects of the so-called Delayed Stress Syndrome;
• BW^{sm} can be applied at home, in the workplace or in any clinical setting to victims of rape, incest, accidents, fire, attempts on one's life, in order to release encapsulated memories, still affecting their lives;
• Introducing SpeyerMethod into prison systems;
• All the above in foreign languages.

"Utopia" need not be "fantasy island" any longer!

Note: To make "helping others" a little more attractive to some volunteers, a strictly regulated small fee may be charged. This will facilitate the process of transference, short as it will be.

Chapter Seven

THE HISTORY OF LIFE AND BRAIN

. . . of Cells and Beings

In order to get an insight into the day-to-day and night-to-night operations of our brain, we will first have to understand its evolutionary path,
eventually coming to this thinking, feeling, dreaming, and physical
apparatus it is, today.

Life first existed on this earth some 2½ billion years ago in some
little known form of spores or particles that came from outer space.
They may have been remnants of burned out stars or planets or just
space debris from the Big Bang happening. They must have contained
compressed bits of essential information of all biological life as we
know it today (DNA).

When these spores arrived on our planet for the first time, they
found pools of water in which they could start the incubating process
which was intrinsic to their nature. They developed later into little
organisms, into bacteria and eventually into cells. Having reached
that point, they could divide themselves in duplicates so that one cell
became two of the same cell.

In the next stage of development two separate cells started to
combine and created together a third living unit. Of that deep, dark
history of life, the human species—which was eventually going to be
the result of that dividing—has no conscious or even subconscious
memory.

In Comparison:

*The human individual of today has no conscious memory of the
time spent in his mother's womb. There, his father's cell and his
mother's cell combined to create a third living unit, thus creating their
offspring.*

To create life there is always the need for a father and a mother cell. You and I were made that way and so were our parents from their parents' cells. And going back—way back—we will find the very first cells that inhabited the earth.

To find where life began, we have to go back to the very first cells that ever lived. It we want to find out who we are—to find our biological roots—we have to find out what happened to that very-first cell that swam in the shallows of the oceans, when life on Earth first came into existence.

These very-first cells lived by themselves but then got sort of lonely and started to cluster together, becoming units.

These units, thrifty and efficient as they were, allocated specialized functions to certain individual cells, in order to save on labor and on energy and to develop better ways of surviving.

Whichever cell was available and best situated to do a certain job was instructed to perform that function for the rest of its life. Eventually, every single cell in that unit received specific instructions. These instructions are now known by such names as DNA, RNA, codes, messages, programs or blueprints. Every cell knows at birth what function to perform and even how long to live.

Here's how cell units developed—over three stages—into biological life forms and how they eventually culminated into H. sapiens, as we know him today.

Cell #1, the Physical Cell

The first units in the history of "the Cell," neither had a system of thinking nor of sensing. These units were thrown back and forth with the flow of the pond they lived in. All they did was to nourish themselves. Soon they found out that this was not too practical. They ran into all kinds of problems, such as temperature changes, light variations, and lack of certain nutrients, all together causing untimely death.

I will call this type of cell, *cell number 1*.

Cell #2, the Sensing Cell

In the next phase of development, cells on the outside of the unit started to learn to observe their environment. They began to notice differences in temperature, in light, and in the salt content of the waters they lived in. Some of these sets of circumstances were less beneficial to their existence than others. They started to react to these negative conditions and found new ways to adapt to them. Because of their capacity to change and to adapt, the previous bad—life-threatening—circumstances could now become their "happy little world." This is known in the trade as survival or mutation.

At a later stage, some of these sensitive cells were born with the capability of receiving a message (signal) from the outside. Once they got the message, they worked with it to the ultimate benefit of the whole unit. It became the most primitive form of sensing, learning, reacting, and programming. These sensitive cells only had one function, and that was to protect their unit against dying. So, in this most primitive form of "thinking," all they could do was to differentiate between life and death, or rather between life and threat-to-life, between good and bad, peace and war. It became the basis for a programmed survival mechanism.

I will call these sensing cells, *Cell number 2*.

Before we continue to look at the make-up and functions of Cell #3, let's first make a comparison of how the development of the human species parallels the development of Cells #1 and #2. I will call these human beings, Beings (= cell) #1 and Beings (= cell) #2.

Beings #1

Some cell units wanted to get acquainted with other cell units. How did they go about it?

Cells—such as the sperm and the egg, for instance—are built like a mail-order catalog. They possess within themselves every part of the entire living unit they belong to. These parts are sort of microphotographed into them. When a micropictured cell of one unit merges with a micropictured cell of another unit, they together form a new unit with its own, combined, catalog.

Just as you order a chair from a picture in a mail-order catalog and get a life-size chair delivered to your home, in the same way you develop life-size arms and legs and the rest of your whole Self, from those micropictures that were in your father's and mother's cells, which made you.

The one cell in the watery broth with which contemporary life started eventually grew into a unit, called fish. Later that fish jumped ashore and called itself, reptile. It learned to fly, became a bird and out of this whole mess of a different kind of "species" came a monkey. That monkey developed into an ape and then, we finally came to a point, when we met the first creatures, who could, more or less, qualify as humans.

We found them in the hottest part of the world, Africa.

Whether you prefer to call these first semi-human Adam and Eve or Pithecanthropuses makes no difference whatsoever.

I will call those animal-people, these humanoids, *Beings #1.*

Compare this period with contemporary human life in the womb.

Beings #2

The following era of the human race is a most primitive one. Those were our pre-caveman days, of which we have little memory, if any memory at all.

This era of the development of the human species must also be compared with the first 1½ years of a baby's life.

The pre-caveman did not have the intelligence to record his own history for posterity. He just nourished from the earth. He found food, he didn't plant it.

A baby doesn't "plant" either and only nourishes from his mother's breast.

Then caveman came, and he started to make observations through his newly developed senses. He told himself what was good and what was bad for his survival. Good or bad were the only differentiations he knew. Things in his life were either black or white, never gray. There was only yes or no, never maybe. Just as cell #2 started sensing, caveman started his own form of sensing, reacting, and learning.

I will call them *Beings #2.*

And now, we'll continue with Cell #3 and compare it with Being #3.

Cell #3

Next stage: from signals to symbols, the thinking cell.

One day, Man started to run into complications. So far, he had only reacted to specific signals. For instance, when water poured down from heaven, he got wet. That was an absolute thing. He lived only by such absolute signals. Only later in his development did his own body and his environment become so complicated, that sometimes a signal did have more than one meaning. It appeared no longer to be absolute. Having arrived at this point, he had to develop a more sophisticated system to survive, a system that could tell him the difference between multi-meaning signals.

If you see a flashing light on a vehicle you know that it could be a police car, or a fire truck, or an ambulance. Signals may have many forms and each form has many possibilities of translation.

To our first man on earth, however, a flashing light could have meant only *one* thing, let's say a fire engine. When all of a sudden, an ambulance appeared in front of him, instead of a fire engine, he was terribly confused. He would have said: "Hey, wait a minute, there is something wrong here. I was supposed to see a fire engine with a flashing light. How come this ambulance has a flashing light as well?" In his mind, the flashing light could only belong to a fire engine, *not* to an ambulance.

As a matter of fact, our little children of today, have the same reactions as the adult caveman.

His experience with multi-meaning signals really set developing Man thinking. At this point, other types of cells started to operate in his brain. They became his conscious reasoning and thinking brain. He now became capable of differentiating. Between black and white, he found a lot of gray. There were a lot of maybes between yes and no. He started to use tools and weapons as extensions of his muscles.

In the same way a little child will become aware of his environment and start to use his muscles to walk and to hold on.

I will call this "thinking" cell, that made it possible for him to adapt to a more complicated environment, *Cell Number 3.*

Beings #3

Man has now entered into a period in which the signal — meaning one thing — has become a symbol, meaning a multiple of things. The need to differentiate developed the need for a thinking brain and this process is manifested as intellect and the power of logic and reasoning. These are the people that populate the earth today.

I will call them *Beings #3.*

We have now reached the point in human development at which Homo sapiens starts to walk on his own power, still a little wobbly though, just as:

The subsequent development of a child, from the age of 1½ till 3½ is called "programming-by-parents." The child is now going through a stage in which he will accept—unconditionally and absolutely—his parents' love and law, in whatever form it may come to him. This love-and-law program will become his lifelong survival-guidance mechanism.

... of Cells and Gods

Compare this with what the human race has similarly done. In its development it accepted the love and law of a god. It its most primitive stages, fathergod was fire, thunder, eruptions, and floods. They all represented *fear*. Mothergod was fertility, creation and sex, all representing *love*. Fathergod, equaling destruction and fear is, in final analysis, *Death*. Mothergod, equaling creation and love is, in final analysis, *Life*.

In the next phase of human development, we find that fathergod-fear and mothergod-love developed into religions.

Fathergod-fear, of the once primitives, developed into Judaism and Mohammedanism, emphasizing law and righteousness, Moses and Mohammed, both, in final analysis, fear and therefore, death.

The mothergod-love of the primitives became the religions of Buddhism and Christianity, emphasizing forgiveness and love, Buddha and Maria, in final analysis, love and therefore, life.

In its further development, we find that, as the child is programmed by his parents . . . so is the human species—at its early age— programmed by religions, as if the Ruling Bodies were his "parents."

What developed from fathergod religion turned out to be fathergod government. It picked up the feargod of the primitives and the lawgod of the religions. It combined those two and manifested itself as restricting, fear-imposing, unforgiving and punishing, all equaling Communism and Fascism.

The mothergod government combined sex with lust and love with chastity, gave unrestricted freedom, protected the rights of the strongest and turned out to be selfish and not having a true interest in Man. It called itself, Capitalism.

Judaism (fathergod) and Christianity (mothergod) are *one*-parent religions.

Communism, Fascism, and Capitalism are *one*-parent governments.

Needless to say, a religion as well as a government taking care of its children, the human population, should consist of both, a father *and* mother type of benevolent, democratic authority.

In the 20th century the human race, having extended its muscles with such tools as bulldozers and nuclear weaponry, also extended its brain power with such brain imitations as radar, television and super computers. It is copying the body's electrical system with such obvious things as electricity and laser.

Almost all bases for inventions can be found in the physical make-up of the human body. As a matter of fact, we could get to know our living brain much better by studying its brainchildren, its inventions.

To summarize:

We, and I mean you and I, have gone through a three-stage development, both in Life-General (cells) as well as in Life-Specific (Man). In our brain, the first stage, *Cell #1* is equal to our body, our instincts, our total *physical* make-up. The cell #1 part of the brain performs actions and reaction, dictated and regulated by instincts and by automatic functions of the body.

Cell #2's part of the brain represents our system of *sensing*. It warns and guides us because its sole function is to keep us from dying. In one word, survival. It is the strongest motivating force we possess and subjugates everything to its force. It has more power than our physical cell, cell #1, and instructs our whole being to stay out of danger. And, believe it or not, it is even stronger than our cell #3, our rational consciousness.

Cell #3's part of our brain is just a newcomer. We only recently started to *"think."* But, as in we will see later in this chapter, cell #3 cannot operate on its own. It is *always* influenced by what cells #1 and #2 have to say about cell #3's "wisdom."

Keep Comparing!

The development of a person, from the moment of conception on, is identical to the development of life on earth. Over billions of years, going through three stages, a human person was produced. Over a period of nine months, the sperm and the egg together, dividing again and again, becoming a fishlike creature in the incubation process, finally producing a human baby.

... of Cells and the Human Species

The development of the human species on Earth and the growth of a human baby goes even further in its similarity.

After a baby is born, it lives only in a physical world, cell #1. It can express itself only physically. It makes sounds but the sounds are incoherent. It moves but its moves are uncoordinated.

When the baby is unhappy, for instance, because it doesn't get enough milk or its doesn't feel the warmth of its mother's body, it cannot say: "Look Ma, I am unhappy. Hold me, darn it." It cannot speak, so it starts to cry, it becomes colicky, gets a rash . . . it talks with its body.

When the baby is about 1½ years old, cell #2 starts to operate. The little boy or girl is now able to react to outside impulses with his own feelings. This period lasts until he is 3½.

This is a very important age for any child. During this period he receives the life or death, black or white, yes or no survival messages. These messages he will learn from people who are nearest to him, usually his father and mother. He will then accept those messages as his norm, for the rest of his life. It will have become his survival kit. Even if he didn't like the messages, he will still accept them as the "holy truth." This learned, parent-programmed survival code becomes his guidance system for his entire walk through life.

At the age of 3½, cell #2 stops taking messages. Rational consciousness starts to take over. All the impressions the child receives from now on will enter his cell #3 part of the brain. He had to activate that part of his brain (#3) because his life, the world around him had become more complicated, due to the fact that he was now capable of observing multi-meaning signals turning into symbols.

As a human being, we live in three dimensions. We have a physical mind in cell #1, we have a subconscious feeling mind in cell #2 and a conscious rational mind in cell #3.

The human hang-up, from time to time, is that we do not seem to be willing to face or to recognize or even want to listen to our own cells #1 and #2. We have an inkling of them and that is as far as we go. Our status quo of thinking seems to be solely vested in cell #3, our "intellect." Most people lived walled-in in cell #3. Not only people as individuals but our culture, our entire state of affairs, seems to idolize intellect per se.

Time has come, whether we like it or not, that we have to start taking notice of our other two dimensions. More so, because they are the actual base of our thinking and behavioral processes, as we will see on the following pages.

And, by the way, look how computers developed . . . compare!

Brain: Computer:
Cell #1 ROM (ready-only memory)
physical fixed programs for automatic tasks
Cell #2 RAM (random access memory)
feeling takes on new information, determines kind and use of
software
Cell #3 DOS (disk-operating-system)
intellect software

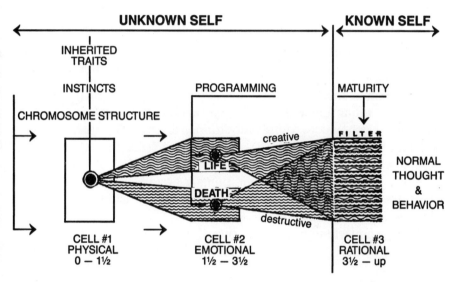

Progressive construction pattern of thought and behavior.

To make a prediction of what the next phase of development of the human race would be, we'll have to look at what happens in the development of a child between the ages of 3½ and 12. We will then observe that the parental programming, the emotional one, has ended. A development, based on intelligence, will begin with the help of a technical specialist, the teacher!

A five-year-old child will learn to read and write in order to get acquainted with himself and with his environment. He learns arithmetic, so that he may organize his awareness in relationship to the world he moves about in.

Awareness of Self and environment in the human race of the twentieth century has become quite apparent in such phenomena as curiosity in Self (psychoanalysis) and in his environment (use of sciences). And in an attempt to throw off the absolute rule of the father and mother gods, the undemocratic governments and religions.

Since the child will now have to look toward his teacher as his main informant...

... the future government will have to have its emphasis on science, rather than on politics.

Just like the old church governments threw off the symbols of the primitives...

... our present political governments threw off the influence of the church.

And so will future science governments throw off politicians.

The human race was programmed with violence, destruction and pain. Its young life was one long struggle against volcanoes, wild animals, earthquakes, rains and storms, diseases, hunger, and the stealing of wives and children. Man had to fight a constant, daily, "life-or-death" battle.

Since programming is unconditionally accepted as norm, as survival, we, the human race of today, are still "attracted" to violence, destruction and pain.

Today, somewhere inside each one of us, we are—to say the least—intrigued by our neighbor's misfortunes, by death, by accidents, fires, and rapes.

We still fight wars, watch wrestling matches and buy newspapers with gory headlines. We read and watch crime stories. We believe in the devil and in hell ...

Mankind is still nourishing its own neuroses.

Walking Through the Brain

Every message that enters the brain is transported into a cell with a certain amount of electricity. This amount is regulated and controlled by instincts, by inherited traits, programming, maturity and by the receptiveness of the moment, mood.

The brain has to release this input, after digestion and storage, into output. In computer language, this is called input-processing-output. Illustration:

A joke makes one laugh. This is an action of input electricity into the cell (the joke), followed by a reaction of output electricity out of the cell (the laugh).

Although the laugh is a very obvious reaction, sometimes reactions are not all that clearly observable. Just thinking about something, for instance, draws electricity into cells.

Another illustration:

Let's say that a person gets into his car at home and plans to drive to the shopping center. The route he plans to take is formed in his brain with a certain amount of input electricity. The moment he has parked his car at the store, this extra amount of electricity is automatically released, used up (output). His brain's assigned task is completed.

One more illustration:

All day long bits and pieces of electricity go in and out of the brain. Sometimes it works quite intricately. While he was driving his car to the shopping center, his brain was constantly measuring distance, objects and speed. All that measuring meant extra electricity in his brain cells. In this case, reactions are almost immediate. Output electricity is sent to his hands and his feet and his car is held in proper position on the road.

In this framework of input and output electricities, the human hang-up is that, at certain times, he is incapable of reacting. In that case, he cannot rid himself of that excess electricity. Thus, traumas are created. Not-reacting may be caused, for instance, when one is afraid, or not allowed, or somehow not capable of reacting.

When this happens during the programming period (0–3½ years) this person will be in real trouble at a later age. He will then have a hang-up.

Our brain is constructed out of three separate parts which are connected to each other—and to the rest of the body—through roadways of electrical/chemical currents. These three parts are the result of the following sequence of development:

Cell #1 First stage of development (0–1½ yrs)	The physical brain; it relates to Man's animal instincts and archetypal primitive memories. (middle brain)
Cell #2 Second stage of development	The subconscious brain; it relates to the memories of the teachings of the parents, during programming years. Right brain survival mechanism.

(1½–3½ yrs)

Cell #3   The conscious brain; it relates to the world we
Third stage   perceive, limited by our senses and extra senses
of development   (left brain)
((3½ years up)

The thinking, acting and general behavior processes of a human being are only possible as the result of a flow of electricity going through these three parts of the brain, in specific directions.

In our thinking process, the flow originates in our physical brain, cell #1. Then it goes through our subconscious brain, cell #2, and finally ends up in our conscious brain, cell #3, where it becomes apparent as thought and behavior.

The reason that the electricity flow follows this particular path—and not another—is due to its historical/biological sequences of development.

However, this particular direction is only followed during the day, or when it is light, when the eyelids are open. During the night, or when it is dark, or when the eyelids are closed, the flow reverses itself. It then goes from cell #3 to #2 and leaves the brain through cell #1. There, it becomes apparent, for instance, in dreaming, making love (orgasm) or recalling. In the SpeyerMethod it is used in order to arrive faster at the location of the trauma. For this very reasons, the subject's eyes are covered during the sessions.

Flow of Electricity in the Brain

Normal flow.

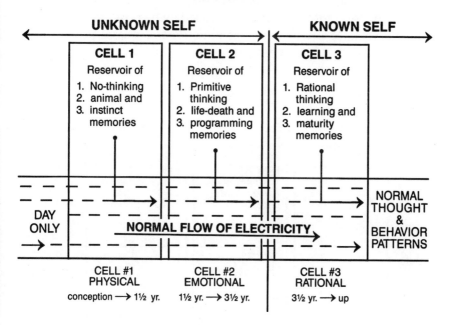

Flow with trauma in cell #1.

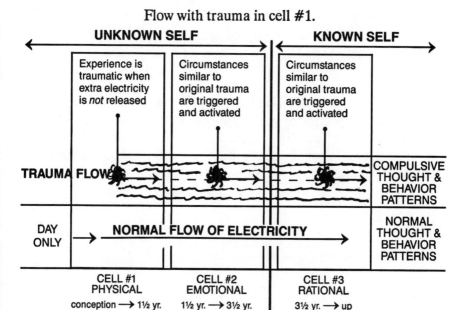

If input is *not* followed by output—if the amount of electricity is not digested or otherwise used up—the electricity, staying within the cell, is causing a problem. It is then called a trauma or stress.

Let's say that the excess electricity in cell #1 was caused by an undigested negative happening between the ages of 0 and 1½. At 1½, cell #1 locks up shop and the extra electricity is trapped. Cells #2 and #3 are now, automatically, influenced by this trauma. It becomes apparent in later life as psychosomatic illness, sexual problems, or problems resulting from a birth trauma.

Flow with trauma in cell #2.

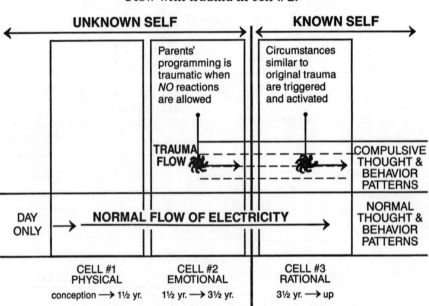

The level in cell #2 is too high, too much input, not enough output during the programming years (1½–3½). Cell #2 closes up at age 3½ and the excess electricity is locked in. Cell #3, our consciousness, in influenced. It usually shows up as an emotional hang-up and/or compulsive behavior.

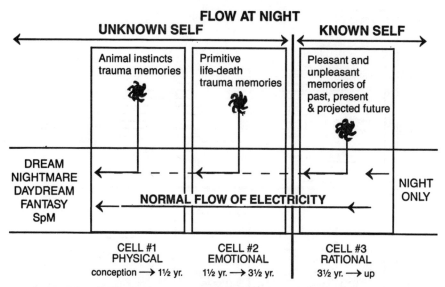

At night, in darkness, or during the day when the eyelids are closed, the inflow of the daytime reverses itself and becomes outflow.

Any cell in our system which holds excess electricity from a trauma or any other undigested information has now a chance to get rid of some, if not all.

This results in such phenomena as nightmares, dreaming, daydreams, fantasies, visions, recalling, or orgasm. Also, while suffering from any physical and/or emotional pain for which one closes one's eyes.

Neurocybernetics

Cybernetics is the guidance-through-feedback system of Life, maintaining, guarding and defending its Norms.

The most essential norm of life is to stay in dynamic balance in order to continue life, steering toward a predetermined, timely death.

Malfunctioning behavior, in cybernetic language, reads as follows: "The inherited biological guidance-through-feedback system is acted against by a foreign, parent-made guidance-through-feedback system, steering in the direction of an *un*timely death."

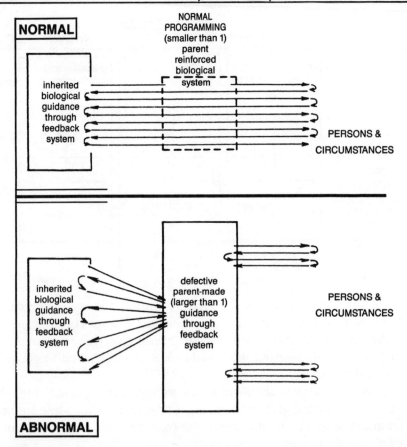

When the strength of the parent-made system becomes stronger (larger) than 1, the original biological system stops operating as an independent guidance system. The original biological norm is then generated and directed toward an abnormality, the parent-made (foreign) norm.

Malfunctional behavior, therefore, is mis-directed "energies."

Lost in Trinity

Illness and Abnormality

It seems that sometimes the 3-part brain does not operate all that properly. Maybe only two parts work and one does not. Or one part works and two do not. Or sometimes one or two parts work part of the time and other times they don't. We're now talking mental illness.

Mental illness is also a physical or genetic abnormality or mistake influencing our thinking and behavioral brain processes.

Shock

Then, there is this sudden traumatic happening called "shock." A form of mental injury caused by a mental accident. A person may receive an unexpected message about the death of a loved one. Or a husband may leave his wife, who still loves him, at a moment's notice (or vice versa, of course). Or, over a period of time, problems are piling up, till the moment comes that there is no way out.

All this type of information comes into Cell #3, our consciousness, with such quantities of electricity (= information), that these cells fill up too much or too fast or too suddenly or all three at the same time. This creates what is commonly known as shock.

Delayed Shock Reaction

Another type of shock, caused by a sudden or continuous fear of death or a strong feeling of loss or disappointment, may not influence the victim's daily thoughts and behavior until many years after the actual traumatic happening(s). Sometimes as much as 20 or 30 years later. At this point in the victim's life, the fear and sometimes the physical pain or ailments connected with the original trauma re-appear without any apparent reason. And a link with the past cause is sometimes difficult to diagnose. The connections with the past are often forgotten and the physician or the psychiatrist is liable to treat only the symptoms. This type of trauma-reappearance—also known as Delayed Stress Syndrome, Post-Traumatic Stress Disorder (PSTD) or KZ syndrome can be observed among combat veterans, ex-prisoners of war and survivors of holocaust and concentration camps. The trauma may also reappear, 20 or 30 years later, among some victims of accidents, rape or even of childhood illnesses, such as polio.

The conditions to cause this delayed traumatic experience must be as follows:

1. The trauma must have occurred and must have been consciously experienced, after the age of 3½.
2. The victim must not have been able to react sufficiently to the imposed fear.

As a consequence of (1) and (2), an extra amount of electricity (= fear) is trapped in Cell #3.

To explain this recurrence, we must turn to the drawing, "The aging of the cell."

DELAYED STRESS SYNDROME

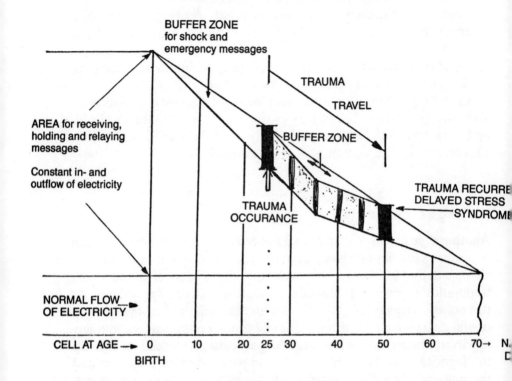

BUFFER ZONE
for shock and
emergency messages

TRAUMA

TRAVEL

AREA for receiving,
holding and relaying
messages

BUFFER ZONE

Constant in- and
outflow of electricity

TRAUMA RECURRE
DELAYED STRESS
SYNDROME

TRAUMA
OCCURANCE

NORMAL FLOW
OF ELECTRICITY

CELL AT AGE → 0   10   20 25 30   40   50   60   70→   N
BIRTH

AGING AND SHRINKING OF THE TRAUMA CELL

Let's assume that the trauma occurred between the ages of 20 and 25. The area of the cell, designated as "Buffer Zone for Shock and Emergency Impressions," has done its job. It has caught the shock and prevented the victim from total collapse or insanity. The "fear-electricity" has filled up the area, pressing against the top of the cell, without actually exploding. Remember, he did not react—condition b, fear, being the powerful inhibitor.

In other words, this trauma remained in the buffer zone with that given quantity of fear electricity.

As the victim aged, the trauma mass started to travel down the age line. As it moved further down, we find empty space appearing again in the top of the buffer zone, above the trauma mass. There is room again for emergencies and everything appears to be normal.

However, when the trauma mass approaches the year 50, it touches the top line again. The trauma re-appears as a pressing problem.

Shock-Reinforced Programming

Yet, it's not all that black and white. The very fact that a person gets a shock from a particular set of circumstances—after the age of 3 ½, condition a—may be a re-enforcement of bad programming before the age of 3 ½. We will have then a combination of bad programming plus reinforcement through *like* circumstances, such as were experienced during that bad programming period.

1. Bill was programmed by a powerful and strict father (0–3½ yrs)	1. John was programmed by a peace-loving and understanding father (0–3½ yrs)
2. During his POW time: Bill had fear of strong male authority figures, the prison guards	2. During his POW time: John did not have particularly strong fears of male authority
3. Bill—due to his father-programming (1) could not release his fears during his POW time	3. John—due to his father-programming (1) did not have any inner fears to speak of
4. 20 years later Bill's POW fears came back as Delayed Stress Syndrome	4. 20 years later John still has bad memories but only when recalled at will

Blockages

Blockage in Cell #3

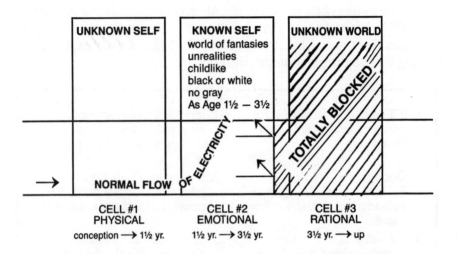

If Cell #3, our consciousness, becomes permanently blocked and the flow of electricity is prevented from taking its normal course, it will then find its way out, through Cell #2, our subconsciousness.

This will cause a person to live in the world of his subconsciousness, a world of childlike fantasies and unrealities. This type of illness is not necessarily always constant. Sometimes it may alternate between the normal-flow-out, Cell #3, and the abnormal-flow-out, Cell #2. Sometimes, the flow even slips its way out through the archetypal memories of Cell #1.

This total phenomenon is known as schizophrenia.

Blockage in Cells #3 and #2

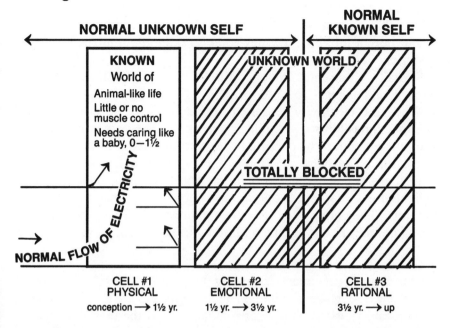

If both cells #3 and #2, are blocked, thoughts and behavior will exit through Cell #1, the physical part of the brain. This person will live in his physical world. He will lead an animal-like existence. He becomes a vegetable and has no control over his muscles, his excreta and lives like an adult baby (idiocy).

In whatever world these people may live, it's always their real world, their reality of that moment. If he goes back to another reality, expressing himself through another part of his brain, he shall not remember his wanderings in the other domains of that same brain. It is "Relative Reality."

Kinetic Brain "Energy"

There are also mental conditions which have nothing to do with blockage and in which a person seems to be perfectly normal. He is not mentally ill or emotionally disturbed. His status is that his personal flow of electricity, going through the three parts of his brain, is constantly too high or constantly too low, or alternates between too high and too low. These expressions of Nature are usually inherited.

If the electricity is permanently too high an extremely strong need for expression is apparent. He is a constant talker, moves hands and feet, can't sit still, can't listen to other people and has a strong sex drive.

His cells, trying to go back to normal level, are constantly pouring out that extra electricity. He is one of those go-getters.

If such a person has, in addition, a bad programming and is as a result thereof inhibited, he may come to sudden outbursts, known as hysterics.

Sexually, these men can go on forever, women roll through one orgasm, climaxing 10 to 15 times.

When the electricity content in the cells is too low, a generally depressed, easily tired attitude is apparent. The person is lethargic and inactive (not to be confused with certain thyroid conditions or as a result of a short-rest reaction of the hyperactives). Sometimes the flow alternates between too high and too low. That person is then delighted with happiness one moment, just to fall back into sadness the next. They are labeled as manic depressives. These phenomena are sometimes also labeled as: Minimal Brain Dysfunction (MBD).

Our brain is the most fascinating "something" that I know of. Walking through its labyrinth, I find its beginnings are shrouded and mystical . . . its end not in sight. Our brain is the umbilical cord, nourishing our curiosity about who we are, where we came from and where we're going.

Chapter Eight

THE "WHO AM I?" GAMES

Do-It-Yourself Analysis Through Analyzing Others

Since do-it-yourself analysis is virtually impossible, we have to get to know ourselves in the first instance through analyzing *others*. It is hardly possible to look at your Self in a purely clinical way. You can never be sure whether your conclusions about your own behavior and thoughts are based on your own fears, your own wishes, or other feelings of which you may not be aware. Even if you are aware of some, you tend to rationalize them as the *general norm*. In other words, you cannot analyze yourself using what *you* feel is the *norm*.

In order to be objective as a self-analyst, you have to know the norm of *every* individual, not only your own. Once you know *all* the individual norms, then you are capable of understanding the *general norm*, including your own.

The purpose of self-analysis is, of course, to get to know yourself and understand those patterns by which you live. The patterns were set in your brain in early childhood, by your parents. They became your survival (guidance) systems and still influence your day-to-day thoughts and behavior, and will, as a matter of fact, for the rest of your life.

If you are the type who has problems in relationships with the opposite sex (or same sex, if you're a homosexual) and can't keep a marriage or a relationship going . . . or if you're the type who has problems in your work, and *your* promotion always seems to go to someone else . . . or if you feel uncomfortable in situations or circumstances in which you really shouldn't . . . take heed:

You will find these two games to be a simple method to discover these basic elementary survival patterns. It will teach you to look at yourself and to look at others from a "survival guidance system" point of view.

You will learn that all your thoughts and behavior are influenced, even dictated, by subconscious commands which you have no way of escaping unless you first get to know them. The process of getting to know these patterns and admitting to yourself that they really exist is sometimes a painful one. Yet, you can't rid yourself of these hang-ups without the pain of looking at yourself in the light of these raw-naked truths. As a normal procedure of self-analysis, you may initially reject the truth, knowing all the time deep within you that those things you have discovered are real.

After you have conjured up enough courage to accept the truth, you will be a happier person with fewer hang-ups. It will then amaze you to find how easy it is to socialize with your family and relatives, to get along in social circles and in your workplace.

In case you are seriously considering starting to work on your own problem and/or to start working with other people as a helper, read and re-read the entire book a couple of times. Below, a few words about the two "games" which are to be found on the following pages.

Getting to Know You: I

This game is really not a game but a proof that human relations are subject to individual parent-programming signals. This is a serious method you can play to decode, to discover, to get an insight into, all kinds of signals of parental programming and all kinds of consequent malfunctional behavior in adult life.

Getting to Know You: II

Going deeper   After you have "analyzed" a fair number of people with the above-mentioned game ("Getting to know you -I-"), you should have acquired a pretty good insight into the human mind and, therefore, into yourself.

In order to deepen your insight, I suggest that you start playing this game (#II) with some more -the same or different-people, preferably strangers, that is to say, no immediate relatives or good friends. The less you know about your subjects, the better the results you get.

It is important, however, that you are alone with your subject and that he/she is willing to let you have a sincere try at "analyzing" him/her.

If the person is afraid or makes a joke out of it, *don't do it*, although this person may be the one who needs it most.

GETTING TO KNOW YOU: I

How to Play, Charts, and Descriptions

First, play the game with a fair number or persons—but not less than 15—one at a time. The less you know about them, the better.

Note: In this game you can *not* decode inherited traits or chromosome structures that influence behavior.

Play the game with anyone who is "game."

1. You start with drawing a triangle, like so:

$$\triangledown$$

2. Write at left-hand upper corner the letter "F" for father:

$$^{F}\triangledown$$

3. Write at right-hand upper corner the letter "M" for mother:

$$^{F}\triangledown^{M}$$

4. Depending on what your subject's sex is, write at bottom "S" for son or "D" for Daughter:

   Note: From this point on, I'll use only "he" or "his" for both, male and female alike.

5. Ask your subject to remember his parents' attitude to him and also toward each other during his early childhood, until the age of 3½. If he cannot produce such memories, let him take them from a later age (till 11 or 12).

   Parents usually don't change that much.

   Now, ask him who –his father or his mother– was the stronger one in the family, the authority. Who was the dominant parent? Was his father stronger (emotionally, of course; we're not talking about body strength) or was his mother the dominant one in the family? *Or*, were they equally strong or equally weak as your subject remembers them? Now, make the following notes on your triangle (choose only *one*):

6. Father "strong" and mother "weak"

$$F^S \bigtriangledown M^W \quad \text{or} \quad F^S \bigtriangledown M^W$$
$$S \qquad\qquad D$$

7. Father "strong" and mother "strong"

$$F^S \bigtriangledown M^S \quad \text{or} \quad F^S \bigtriangledown M^S$$
$$S \qquad\qquad D$$

8. Father "weak" and mother "strong"

$$F^W \bigtriangledown M^S \quad \text{or} \quad F^W \bigtriangledown M^S$$
$$S \qquad\qquad D$$

9. Father "weak" and mother "weak"

$$F^W \bigtriangledown M^W \quad \text{or} \quad F^W \bigtriangledown M^W$$
$$S \qquad\qquad D$$

Throughout the entire game we will use the terms "cold" and "warm." *Cold* means: Critical, uninterested, fear, no emotional contact, no communication, restrictions, punishments, and absence of parents. *Warm* means: affectionate, understanding, loving, and in general good emotional contact and communication.

When making these notes on your triangle, write them as follows: "cd" for cold and "wm" for warm.

10. According to your subject's impression, at the age from 0 to 3½, how was the relationship between his father and his mother? "Cold" or "Warm"?

$$F^S \xrightarrow{cd} M^W \quad F^S \xrightarrow{wm} M^W$$
$$\bigtriangledown \qquad \bigtriangledown$$
$$S \qquad\quad D$$

Add "cd" or "wm" on the top line of the triangle between F and M.

11. According to his impression, how was the relationship between him and his father? Warm or cold?

$$F^S \xrightarrow{cd} M^W \quad F^S \xrightarrow{wm} M^W$$
$${}_{wm}\bigtriangledown \qquad {}_{cd}\bigtriangledown$$
$$S \qquad\quad D$$

Add "wm" or "cd" to the left leg of your triangle between the points "F" (father) and your subject, either "S" (son) or "D" (daughter).

12. How was the relationship between him and his mother? Warm or cold? Add "wm" or "cd" to the right leg of your triangle between the point "M" (mother) and subject, either "S" (son) or "D" (daughter).

$$F^S \underset{wm}{\swarrow}\underset{cd}{\searrow} M^W \quad F^S \underset{cd}{\swarrow}\underset{wm}{\searrow} M^W \quad F^S \underset{wm}{\swarrow}\underset{wm}{\searrow} M^S \quad F^W \underset{cd}{\swarrow}\underset{cd}{\searrow} M^S$$
$$\underset{S}{} \quad\quad \underset{D}{} \quad\quad \underset{S}{} \quad\quad \underset{D}{}$$

13. If there was *no father* or no father figure from age 0 to 3½ or the father wasn't there long enough to be remembered, then we get the following triangle: Instead of putting an "F" for father, we put a sign like this –"⊗"– for no father.

$$\otimes \underset{wm}{\searrow} M^W \quad \otimes \underset{cd}{\searrow} M^S$$
$$\underset{S \cdot \,'}{} \quad\quad \underset{D}{}$$

14. There was almost always a mother or a mother figure.

15. Sometimes there were two father figures at the same time, such as father and a live-in grandfather or uncle. Or sometimes two father figures, one following the other, as in a father followed by a stepfather.

It must all have happened before 3½ years of age.

Now we get the following triangle:

$$F\ F \underset{cd}{\searpoon} \quad\quad F\ F \underset{wm}{\searpoon}$$
$$\underset{S}{} \quad\quad\quad \underset{S}{}$$

16. Or two mother figures: Mother and grandma, housemaid, or stepmother (as in step 15).

$$M\ M \underset{cd}{\searpoon} \quad\quad M\ M \underset{wm}{\searpoon}$$
$$\underset{S}{} \quad\quad\quad \underset{S}{}$$

It's really not all that different from computer programming. Now start looking for *his* triangle on the chart beginning on page 182 for *son* and on page 183 for *daughter*. Find the correct number and read his "destiny."

Note: While reading his chart to him, keep this in mind: All words used in the descriptions on the chart—such as authority, authoritative, relationship, domineering, interest, distant, cold warm, strong, weak, secure, insecure or vague—have only *emotions* as a base.

Imitating a parent means imitating such phenomena as tone of voice, grin on face, grimaces, walk, posture of total body or parts thereof, habits, body language, dress, and also certain symptoms such as coughing and vomiting.

SON

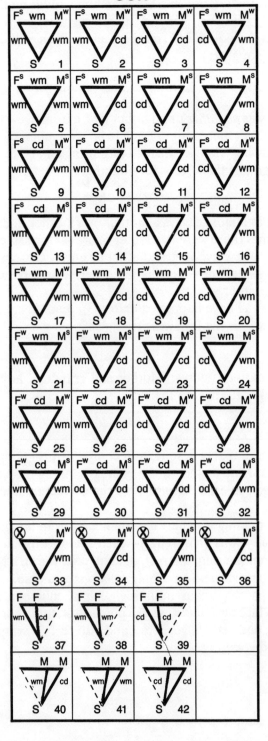

DAUGHTER

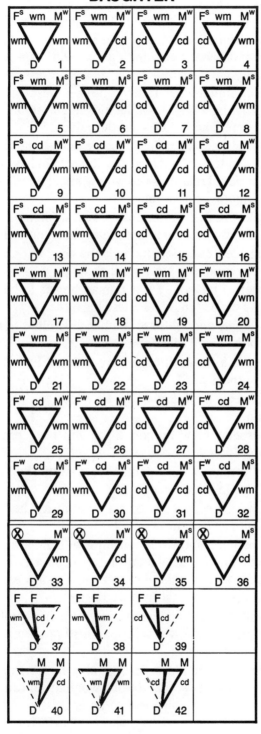

Son

S1. Ideal situation, only limited by inherited traits and circumstances beyond his control; will be a warm and happy man in warm and loving surroundings; he will respect honest male authority.

S2. He will imitate his father; he will respect honest male authority; he will have difficulties in emotional relationships with women; he will be secretly jealous.

S3. He will imitate his father to some degree; he will fear, or be aggressive toward, male authority; he will have difficulties in his emotional relationships with women; he will feel the need to dominate a cold woman.

S4. He is secure in his relationship with women; he is aggressive toward and at the same time fears male authority.

S5. A near-ideal situation; he feels the need to be with a woman who is emotionally stronger than he is.

S6. In order to feel love for a woman he has to have a sense of fear of her; he tends to imitate his father.

S7. He is lonely and feels sad; he has difficulties in relationships with men as well as with women.

S8. He needs a warm domineering woman; he hates and fights male authority.

S9. He respects male authority; he needs to dominate a warm woman.

S10. He respects male authority; he will have problems in his relationships with women.

S11. He is afraid of, yet fights, male authority; he will have problems in relationships with women.

S12. He is afraid of, yet fights, male authority; he has a need to dominate a warm woman.

S13. He can have good relationships with men as well as with women, but not if a man and a woman are together, for instance, as a couple, whether the ties are emotional or in business/professional surroundings.

S14. He will respect male authority; he has problems in his relationships with women, manifesting themselves through fear and/or aggression.

S15. He is a lonely and lost person, either he fears or is aggressive toward men as well as toward women; he can't find "true" love; he challenges people to be aggressive toward him; he has his own secret world, sometimes one of unrealities and fantasies.

S16. He must feel fear in order to sense love; he will be happy with a strong and domineering woman who will regard him as her property; he will fight and/or fear male authority.

S17. A near-ideal situation; he can't stand cold or aggressive people; he is often a dreamer.

S18. He feels secure in a non-aggressive male community; he is not very much interested in woman, perhaps only sexually.

S19. He feels that he is cut off from society; he feels that nobody can ever love him, that nobody cares; he is a very lonely person.

S20. He likes a good relationship with a warm woman; he has absolutely no respect for male authority.

S21. He is greatly influenced by domineering women; he does not think much of male authority.

S22. He is bound to imitate his father; he fears yet is attracted to female authority.

S23. He tries to please male authority; he fights female authority but somehow always loses.

S24. He is jealous of other men; he needs and respects a woman who is warm yet authoritative; there is a possible basis for homosexual tendencies.

S25. He can have good relationships with non-authoritarian men and women; he fears authority; he cannot see a family as one unit but sees each member as a separate entity.

S26. He does not see his family as one unit but sees each member as a separate entity; he does not show emotion to a woman; he likes men who are not authoritative.

S27. He does not see his family as one unit but sees each member as a separate entity; it is difficult for him to relate emotionally to men as well as to women.

S28. He does not see his family as one unit but can only see each member as a separate entity; he feels superior to other men but sees women as his equal.

S29. He can only love a woman who is emotionally much stronger than he is; he may be impotent; he can relate well to men but cannot accept their authority.

S30. He has fear of, but is at the same time attracted to, a domineering woman, he does not respect male authority.

S31. He rejects male authority; he fears yet is attracted to a domineering woman.

S32. He feels attracted to a woman who is emotionally stronger than he is; he cannot accept male authority; a possible base for bisexuality or homosexuality.

Note: The following triangles, 33 through 36, have this in common: He has difficulty in relating to male authority; he either accepts it without criticism or he will fight against it.

S33. He can only love a woman who has a lot of emotional warmth; when in love he cannot stand other men to be around; he is overly jealous, even if another man as much as looks at his wife. + Note above.

S34. He fears an emotionally warm woman; first he is attracted to her then he runs away from her. See note.

S35. He is attracted to a domineering woman; he cannot accept male competition; there is a possible basis for bisexuality or homosexuality. See note.

S36. He fights, yet is attracted to, domineering women; it is possible that he himself is emotionally cold; he lives in his own world, sometimes a world of fantasy. See note.

Note: The following triangles, 37–42, do not take the missing parent into consideration, only the double parent situation. They should be viewed in addition to the appropriate one Father–one Mother triangle.

S37. In his relationship to men he will always need two authority figures next to each other at the same time; one will always be the good one and the other will always be the bad one; in addition there is often an age difference between those two authority figures, one old, one young. + Note above.

S38. He always has good relationships with all kinds of men. See note.

S39. He wants to fight all men all the time; he has a fear of being attacked by every man he meets. See note.

S40. He must always love two women at the same time; he must have a warm woman to love and, at the same time, he must know or love a cold (distant) woman (warm or cold may be reversed). See note.

S41. He must love two warm women at the same time, never only one; he may have his "second" woman in reality or create her in his fantasy. See note.

S42. He thinks all women are bad; he can only love a cold woman; he needs a woman primarily for sex. See note.

Daughter

D1. Ideal situation only limited by inherited character traits and circumstances beyond her control; she is a warm and happy woman in warm and loving surroundings; she will respect beneficent male authority.

D2. She can have good relationships with men; however, she may be jealous and in general will despise, and sometimes even hate, women.

D3. She feels easily rejected; she is lonely and can't seem to find happiness in life; therefore she will always carry with her feelings of envy.

D4. She is attracted to cold men but feels unhappy about it at the same time; she will imitate her mother.

D5. A near-ideal situation: She is confident of her own strength; she feels equal to any man.

D6. She has good relationships with men; she will feel threatened by other women; in general she will be aggressive toward authoritative women.

D7. She feels lonely and sad; she has difficulties in her emotional relationships with men, as well as with women.

D8. She has difficulties in relating to men; she is attracted to men who reject her; she will possibly imitate her mother.

D9. She will respect male authority; she may despise women.

D10. She feels attracted to a strong, domineering man; she has no interest in women; she has no girlfriends.

D11. She fears, yet is attracted to, cold authoritative men; she feels insufficient as a woman.

D12. She fears, yet is attracted to, cold, authoritative men; she will have good relationships with non-aggressive and non-authoritarian women.

D13. She has good relationships with men as well as with women, but not if a man and a women belong together, such as a married couple or in a business or professional setting.

D14. She will have good relationships with strong men; she cannot stand authoritative women.

D15. She is a lonely person and feels sad; she has either a fear of, or is aggressive toward, men and women; she never seems to be able to find love; she will challenge people to become aggressive toward her; she lives often in a secret world, sometimes made up of unrealities and fantasies.

D16. She needs to feel a fear of a man in order to sense love; she will be attracted to men who are strong, cold, and domineering, yet she will always feel rejected; she needs a motherly girlfriend to whom she will listen.

D17. A near-ideal situation: She can't stand cold or aggressive people; she is often a dreamer.

D18. She feels happy with a warm, non-authoritarian man; she will be a little jealous from time to time; women do not interest her.

D19. She feels rejected, shut out; she feels that nobody will ever love her, that nobody cares; she is a lonely woman.

D20. She feels attracted to, and is at the same time miserable with, vague, distant, or cold men; she will imitate her mother.

D21. She will love a warm yet distant man; she will try to dominate him; she will ask authoritative women for advice.

D22. She will like a man who is warm yet distant; she will dominate this man; she doesn't like authoritative women.

D23. Actually she despises men, but yet is attracted to cold, weak men; she is envious of authoritarian women.

D24. She feels attracted to authoritative women; she does not have much regard for men; there is a possible base for lesbian tendencies.

D25. She likes men and women who are warm and weak; she cannot see her family as one unit; she can only see each member as a separate entity.

D26. She cannot see her family as one unit; she can only see each member as a separate entity; she likes weak men; women do not interest her at all.

D27. She does not feel part of her own family; she is lonely, turned within herself; has no good relationships with men or women; she despises authority.

D28. She does not see her family as one unit; she has difficulties relating to weak men but cannot relate to strong men either; she needs a warm but weak girlfriend.

D29. She feels secure in her relationship with a warm but weak man; she can relate well to authoritarian women on a non-emotional basis (professional or business).

D30. She feels secure in her relationship with a warm but weak man; she is afraid of authoritarian women.

D31. She is a lonely woman and feels miserable about her own life; she is afraid of domineering women; she is insecure in all her relationships.

D32. Men don't mean much to her; she will be impressed by a woman who is warm and authoritative; there is a possible basis for lesbian tendencies.

D33. She has no real image of what a man should be; she can fall in love, head over heels, or spontaneously reject, just about any type of man—good-looking or ugly, young or old; she will never be sure of her love feelings; she will always be looking for the "ideal" man, never to find him.

D34. Same as D33; in addition, she feels lonely and is turned within herself.

D35. Same as D33; there is a possible basis for lesbian feelings.

D36. Same as D33; she is often fearful and angry.

Note: The following triangles, 37–42, do not take the missing parent into consideration, only the double parent situation. These numbers should also be viewed in addition to the appropriate one father–one mother triangle.

D37. In her relationship with men she will always feel the need for two authoritative men, together at the same time, a "good" one and a "bad" one, sometimes combined with age. For instance, a young-bad and an old-good, or vice versa. + Note above D37.

D38. In her relationship with men she will always feel the need for two authoritative men, both at the same time; both men are good; she loves both equally; sometimes one is much older than the other. See note.

D39. In her relationships with men she will always feel the need for two cold, authoritative men at the same time; she gets tired of hoping for warmth; she is lonely and creates her own situations of being rejected by men. See note.

D40. In her relationship to women she will always feel the need to have two girlfriends, one warm and one cold; sometimes one is much older than the other. See note.

D41. She will have good relationships with warm women; she will have lots of warm girlfriends. See note.

D42. She will despise all women, regardless of reality; she will never have a girlfriend; she will fear, yet in a way be attracted to all types of authoritative women. See note.

GETTING TO KNOW YOU: II

How to Play, Charts, and Descriptions

Going Deeper   After you have "analyzed" about 15 people (the more the better) with the game on the preceding pages, you should have gotten a pretty good insight into them and into yourself. In order to deepen your insight, I suggest that you start "playing this game" with some more—the same or different—people, preferably strangers, that is to say, no immediate relatives or good friends. The less you know about your subject, the better results you get.

It is important, however, that you are alone with your subject and that he/she is willing to let you have a sincere try at "analyzing" him/her.

If he is afraid, or makes a joke out of it *don't do it*, even if *he* is the one who needs it most.

You start by taking an ordinary sheet of paper (8½×11), and creating the following chart:

NAME: DATE:	(A) FATHER	(B) MOTHER	(C) SELF
(1) ANIMAL	A1	B1	C1
(2) WELL-KNOWN PERSON	A2	B2	C2
(3) MOST IRRITATING	A3	B3	–
(4) HOME	A4	B4	–

The first thing you do is to make sure that your subject has lived the first four or five years of his life under more or less normal family circumstances. There must have been a family unit consisting of father-mother-child-house. (House or home includes brothers, sisters and others, if any.)

If your subject keeps telling you that he has no memories of his childhood, then take his memories of later years. As mentioned before, the parents' attitude doesn't change all that much as the years go by. But be aware: Someone who has no memories whatsoever is sometimes blocking out some nasty childhood experiences.

(A) Father In case there was *no father*, but instead another person such as a live-in grandfather, a stepfather, a much older brother or mother's boyfriend who lives in, make note in square (A) *father* accordingly, marking the name of the substitute father.

NAME: DATE:	(A) No Father Uncle Joe	

In case there was another male person in the house *in addition* to the father such as a live-in grandfather, make a note in square (A) *father* accordingly. There is a strong possibility of a double father image.

NAME: DATE:	(A) Father & Grandpa	

Also make notes in the (A) *father* square if the father died or disappeared during that early period. If a void of males followed, or if he was replaced by one or by many, make notes accordingly in square (A) *father*. Make a note of your subject's age when such changes took place.

NAME: DATE:	(A) Father died Stepfather Bill	

(B) Mother Ask for the same information about the mother (and other women) as you did about the father (and other men):

NAME: DATE:		(B) No Mother Grandma

Another woman *in addition* to the mother, such as a live-in grandmother or a maid may create a double mother image.

NAME: DATE:		(B) Mother & Aunt Lisa

In case of the death of the mother, or if she somehow disappeared from the home scene and was followed, either by a void or by a replacement of one or many women, note it on your chart.

NAME: DATE:		(B) Mother died Stepmother Anne

(A) + (B) Father + Mother   If your subject moved a lot during his programming years, make a note accordingly. (Moving a lot means 4 to 10 times in his first four years.) This will show up as a "moving habit" in his later life.

NAME: DATE:	(A) 0-5 years moved 7 times	(B) 0-20 years moved 13 times

A1 Animal   You will now ask the following question: "Think about your father, when you were little. Look at him with your eyes closed. Now identify him with an animal. What sort of an animal would he be? Say the first animal that comes to your mind. Don't hesitate and don't think."

At first, he will find it an impossible question. He may say: "I don't know; that's very difficult. I never thought about that."

Don't comment on his remarks. Just sit there and wait until he finally comes up with a name of an animal.

Of course, there are others who blurt out the name of an animal right away.

Write the name of the animal down in column A1.

Let's say that your subject said: "Bear." Then your next question will be: "What makes your father a bear?" He will now answer: "Well, he is grumpy, big . . ." He will come up with some physical likeness between his father and the bear.

Write his answers down in single words, *his* words, not yours. Then continue: "What else makes your father a bear?"

This time, he will start to mention some emotional characteristics of his father, such as: "He used to be mean to me" or "He never listened to me" or "He criticized me all the time."

These are the remarks you are really interested in. Write them down in simple words such as: Cruel, cold, strict, critical, doesn't listen, no interest, no affection, always gone, can't talk to him, no communication. But make sure to use his words. *You* must not have an opinion. Don't comment on and don't discuss what he mentions. Don't feed him any suggestions. It all has to come from him. You just sit there, like a machine, taking notes on your paper.

	(A) FATHER
(1) ANIMAL	Bear-grumpy mean-big-cruel doesn't listen-strict no affection

A2 Well-Known Person "Identify your father with a well-known famous or infamous person." Generally, names from the Bible, from history, the movies, TV, sports, politics, etc., will come up. In case he hesitates, you may, in this case alone, suggest these categories to him, He may also mention the name of a teacher or of a local personality. After some thinking, he may say: "Abraham Lincoln." "What makes him an Abraham Lincoln?" you ask.

Here again, he may start to mention a physical likeness but you are only interested in emotional likenesses, such as: "He rules the family." Write down: "rules." When he mentions, as his choice, someone like "Adolf Hitler," you "know" immediately that his father was a cruel man. But wait. Not necessarily so! Your evaluation might have been wrong, because there is always that possibility that your subject admires Adolf Hitler, in which case you have gotten an entirely different pictures of him. It is so *important* to let *him* "do the talking" and not do any interpreting yourself.

Generally, your subject will now repeat or add to the information he gave you above in A1. Write it all down in column A2.

	(A) FATHER
(1) ANIMAL	Bear, etc.
(2) WELL-KNOWN PERSON	Abraham Lincoln rules, criticizes

A3 Most Irritating   When his flow of thoughts has stopped, you ask him: "Which were the most irritating things your father did to you when you were little?" He will accentuate the above. Note in the column A3.

(1) ANIMAL	Bear, etc.
(1) WELL-KNOWN PERSON	Abraham Lincoln, etc.
(3) MOST IRRITATING	Anger, criticizes not allowed to speak

A4 Home   The following question has to do with his father in the home.

"How was your father at home, when you were little?" Here you are interested in such remarks as: "There were always arguments between father and mother" or " He was away from home a lot" or "He beat everybody" or "He was drunk all the time" or "He was a fanatic about cleanliness" or "He was finicky about money."

Write his answers in column A4

We are not particularly interested in his father's good habits and good characteristics because they don't usually cause hang-ups in later life. They do, however influence your subject to the same degree as the bad ones, but the habits they create are non-compulsive habits.

	(A) FATHER
(1) ANIMAL	Bear, etc.
(1) WELL-KNOWN PERSON	Abraham Lincoln, etc.
(3) MOST IRRITATING	Anger, etc.
(4) HOME	No Money — Arguments with mother — Away from home a lot

(B) Mother   The same questions, 1, 2, 3, and 4 are asked about your subject's *mother* and noted in column (B).

In this case, however, you may get an animal like a "lamb," a "cow," or a "cat."

As a famous person, for instance: "Elizabeth Taylor" or "Joan Collins."

Once in a great while your subject may choose a male as a mother figure. Just write it down and find out what it means to *him/her*.

Then ask: *"What* makes your mother a cow?" *"What* makes your mother a Joan Collins?"

Disregard physical likeness, always look for emotional likeness.

NAME: DATE:	(A) FATHER	(B) MOTHER	(C) SELF
(1) ANIMAL	Bear, etc.	Cow—always busy in the kitchen—no communication— no affection	Eagle— fly away— free to do things
(2) WELL-KNOWN PERSON	Lincoln etc.	Joan Collins— mean streak— doesn't listen— 'babbles'	President of the U.S.—rule people—have it my way
(3) MOST IRRITATING	Anger, etc.	has no time for me	—x—
(4) HOME	no money etc.	afraid of father— always cooking and cleaning	—x—

(C) Self The third column is about the subject himself. Ask him only about the animal and famous person, questions 1 and 2.

Tell him to mention his ideal, most attractive, animal and the most respected and admired person he would like himself to be. Note his answers in column (C)1 and 2.

This is where his never-to-be-fulfilled wishes enter the picture. This is where you find out how he wishes to see himself ideally, or in the future. This often turns out to be a more or less accurate gut-feeling of things to come.

* * *

Decoding

Look out for These General Rules before Decoding

Father-Daughter It is important to learn from your *female* subject whether her father was affectionate and warm, or cold and distant. Either attitude will have set the same pattern in all her present-day love relationships.

Mother-Son The same holds true for mother-son. Cold or warm patterns will show up in his later love life. Mother is cold equals love must be cold. Mother = warm means love = warm.

Father-Son You may look to see if his father was strict and critical or did allow his son to express himself and was understanding. Either attitude will show in his attitude toward his boss, his superiors, and others he may have to respect, including the "law of the land."

Mother-Daughter If the mother is a loving wife and friend of her
husband, the daughter will almost certainly be the same with her
husband or lover in her later life.

If the mother is cold and distant to her daughter, she may grow up
to be an "independent" woman and will prefer to work with men
rather than with women.

Decoding the Problem

In order to decode the information on your sheet, you will have to start
out from these basics:

> *Code One*: I love my father—I love my mother
> *Code Two*: *Father* equals *men* in later life
>   *Mother* equals *women* in later life
> *Code Three*: *Wish for the unobtainable* (but only in relationships of
>   love and work.)

> *Note:* You will eventually start to notice that many of your subjects live
> in a *"wish world".*
>
> If there happens to be a 5-step pattern in someone's brain, as
> illustrated on pages 6 through 10, he will wish for an ideal situation
> involving his parents but will never have gotten it!
>
> In adult life he will live with a similiar constant wish for an "ideal"
> relationship or situation. Yet, he never makes it or, if he does, he'll
> destroy it or run away from it. The child/parent pattern repeats itself
> throughout life.

The Explanation

Now you are going to show the person with whom you're playing these
"games" why he has certain attitudes toward men and women that he
never realized he possessed. He always thought that this was the way it
was supposed to be. He thought that what was *his* norm was the same
for everyone.

In some cases, of course, he will deny the correctness of your
explanation. You must know however, that there is always a perfect
balance between his programming (0–3½) years) and his thoughts and
behavior in later life. If you run into an imbalance between the two,

you have to start digging a little more deeply. Eventually you will find that the patterns on your sheet are the correct ones. If someone who has a "cold" parent tells you that he does like affection, then that is certainly true. The hang-up, however, is that he cannot cope with the affection in spite of that fact that he likes it. Admitting these things is painful.

Example #1

THE INFORMATION (from male subject)

NAME: DATE:	(A) FATHER	(B) MOTHER	(C) SELF
(1) ANIMAL	"Bear." Has no time for me. Orders me around. Afraid of him. I fight him but lose. No communication. Cold. Etc.		

THE DECODING (from male subject) in all cases start with "I love my father/mother."

	ACTION — "I DO" (son to father)
1.	"I LOVE MY FATHER" (subject's action)
3.	I fight him
5.	I lose the fight

	REACTION — "I EXPECT" (father to son)
2.	He orders me around (father's reaction)
4.	No communication between us

Father Equals Men in Later Life   Subject will act in his adult life according to pattern "I *do*," 1, 3, 5. Any man he has to respect, he will fight to lose.

Subject will expect (projection) all men to act according to pattern 2, 4, "I *expect*." He expects to be ordered around and he will not communicate.

At the same time, he will express his never-to-be fulfilled wish for understanding and caring male persons.

Example #2

THE INFORMATION (from female subject)

NAME: DATE:	(A) FATHER	(B) MOTHER	(C) SELF
(1) ANIMAL	"Prairie dog." Cold. No communication. Rules me. Afraid of him.		

THE DECODING (from female subject) in all cases start with "I love my father/mother."

	ACTION — "I DO" (daughter to father)
1.	"I LOVE MY FATHER" (subject's action)
3.	I am afraid, I run
5.	I don't talk either

	REACTION — "I EXPECT" (father to daughter)
2.	He is cold, mean, no communication (father's reaction)
4.	He rules me

Father Equals Men in Later Life   Subject will act in her later life according to pattern 1,3,4, "I *do*." I am afraid of the man I love; I run away from him; I do not communicate. She will expect (projection) all men to be cold, mean, to want to rule her and by non-communicative, all according to pattern 2,4, "I *expect*." At the same time. She well express her never-to-be-fulfilled wish for an understanding, loving, and caring man.

Example #3

THE INFORMATION (from male subject)

NAME: DATE:	(A) FATHER	(B) MOTHER	(C) SELF
(1) ANIMAL		"Cow." No communication. No affection. Always busy in the kitchen.	

THE DECODING (from male subject) in all cases start with "I love my father/mother."

	ACTION — "I DO" (son to mother)
1.	"I LOVE MY MOTHER" (subject's action)
3.	I go after her
5.	I give up trying

	REACTION — "I EXPECT" (mother to son)
2.	She doesn't hear me (mother's reaction)
4.	She goes to the kitchen

Mother Equals Women in Later Life   Subject will act in his later life according to patern "I *do*," 1, 3, 5. Any woman he loves, likes, or has to respect he pursues, but "knows" that he can't get her (projection) and gives up.

Subject expects all women to be according to pattern 2, 4, "I *expect*." He expects a woman not to listen to him, that she intends to go and do "something else." She will always be leaving him.

At the same time, he will be expressing his never-to-be-fulfilled wish for a loving caring woman.

Example #4

THE INFORMATION (from female subject)

NAME: DATE:	(A) FATHER	(B) MOTHER	(C) SELF
(1) ANIMAL		"Cat." Jealous of me and Dad. Afraid of her. Accuses falsely.	

THE DECODING (from female subject) in all cases start with "I love my father/mother."

	ACTION — "I DO" (daughter to mother)		REACTION — "I EXPECT" (mother to daughter)
1.	"I LOVE MY MOTHER" (subject's action)	2.	She is jealous (mother's reaction)
3.	I am afraid of her	4.	I feel guilty
5.	I run away		

Mother Equals Women in Later Life   Subject will act in her later life according to pattern "I *do*," 1, 3, 5. She is afraid of women she likes or has to respect. She leaves them. Subject will expect (projection) that all women are jealous of her—according to pattern 2, 4, "I *expect*." This also interferes in her love relationships because she will always expect "the other woman" to come between her and her lover.

After you have experimented with a number of people—the more the better—you should have a pretty good idea of how these patterns work in others. Now, take a good and honest look at yourself.

ABOUT THE AUTHOR

Simon Speyer was born in Amsterdam, the Netherlands, in 1922. He attended the International Kaiser Wilhelm Schule and by the age of 10 spoke four languages fluently. Already at an early age, he lived the life of an unorthodox "adventurer-in-thinking"—as many of his contemporaries called him then. That "aura" has stayed with him throughout his life. Powered by a restless, sharp-analytical and, above all, logical mind, he pursued studies in psychology, criminology, philosophy, art history, languages and philology, taking him to colleges in England and France.

As for so many, the onset of World War II interrupted his studies. When the German Armies occupied Holland, he fled to England in a hectic and daring lifeboat escape across the North Sea. Subsequently, he saw combat in the Dutch East Indies (now Indonesia), where he was captured to become a POW of the Japanese for more than 3½ years.

Fate—literally—threw Speyer into a group of POWs who were academicians of the Dutch infrastructure, doing military service at the time when the Japanese invaded Dutch territory. Speyer recounts: "Here, in this jungle camp [Sumatra], I got the education of my life. Here, I got acquainted with psychoanalysis and Freud, taught by a physician; the religions of the world and Jesus, taught by a minister; chemistry by a chemist; art and music by a musician of a stranded Dutch symphony orchestra; the concept of splitting atoms and Einstein, taught by a physicist. The last two years in the jungle were hell: starvation, illness, daily tortures ... most of us died. I barely made it."

Postwar, he resumed his studies in Holland where he specialized in efficiency engineering and industrial psychology at a corporate management institute. He emigrated to the United States in 1950. He has since become a U.S. citizen. In New York City, Speyer was employed as a psychological consultant, profiling and evaluating executives of companies that were considered potential takeover targets (1952).

By 1956, Speyer had established his own "Human Relations Consultants" office, engaging in market research and executive counseling. Since the early 1960s Speyer had begun to develop his own method

201 *Know Yourself, Heal Yourself*

of evaluating corporate officers. In that process, he also counseled unbalanced—and sometimes stressed—executives back to health. It was from this counseling that the SpeyerTherapy evolved (1963).

In 1964, Speyer was invited to open a practice in London by two prominent Harley Street doctors. During a lifetime of experience as a self-taught theorist and practitioner in the field of the neurosciences, Speyer's research projects have also included working with the "poor and primitives" in East Africa and in Haiti, as well as with the "rich and famous" in Miami and Las Vegas. These three research projects contributed greatly to Speyer's later methods and consulting in the field of the brain sciences.

From the mid-1960s to the early '70s, Speyer practiced his newly developed 10-day, 1½-hour-a-day, SpeyerTherapy in Las Vegas, in which period he wrote his first book about the therapy and specific brain functions, involving malfunctional behavior. This book was first published in the Netherlands and Belgium, in 1972. Two more books followed, one of which became a best-seller.

As a result of his writings, he was invited to introduce his SpeyerTherapy at the University of Leiden in the Netherlands, through the intermediary of Professor Dr. Jan Bastiaans, M.D., head of the Department of Psychiatry (now retired). Subsequently, Speyer was invited by the Catholic University of Leuven (KUL) to introduce his SpeyerTherapy in Belgium. There, he worked with Professor Dr. Steven De Batselier, Faculty of Law, Department of Criminology (1974).

Simultaneously, Speyer developed a method to teach lay people to become full-fledged psychotherapists, also in 10 (full) days. Needless to say that this therapy caused—to say the least—some concern among the established counseling professions. Today, 15 years later, SpeyerTherapy is a well-established therapy in Europe, recognized by government agencies and insurance companies alike.

Back in the United States, Speyer received his Ph.D. from Columbia Pacific University (1978). C.P.U. is a well-known and respected non-traditional university. In his own words, Speyer acclaims: "I was educated in a non-traditional kind of way. This system of granting authorized degrees, based—in the first instance—on work experience in the field accoladed my professional achievements."

Speyer developed his self-help methods in Europe and in America. It became the basis for SpM I and II, as well as for Brain Science in the Workplace (BW^{sm}) and culminated in *Know Yourself, Heal Yourself*. As Speyer Therapy turned out to be the breakthrough of the 1970s, his new work will no doubt result in the breakthrough of the '90s.